kitchen doctor
asthma
cooking for health

kitchen doctor
asthma
cooking for health

foods to combat the symptoms
of asthma and soothe the effects of
eczema and hayfever with 50 recipes

brigid mcconville

southwater

This edition is published by Southwater

Southwater is an imprint of Anness Publishing Ltd
Hermes House, 88–89 Blackfriars Road, London SE1 8HA
tel. 020 7401 2077; fax 020 7633 9499
www.southwaterbooks.com; info@anness.com

UK agent: The Manning Partnership Ltd, 6 The Old Dairy, Melcombe Road, Bath BA2 3LR;
tel. 01225 478444; fax 01225 478440; sales@manning-partnership.co.uk

UK distributor: Grantham Book Services Ltd,
Isaac Newton Way, Alma Park Industrial Estate, Grantham, Lincs NG31 9SD;
tel. 01476 541080; fax 01476 541061; orders@gbs.tbs-ltd.co.uk

North American agent/distributor: National Book Network,
4501 Forbes Boulevard, Suite 200, Lanham, MD 20706;
tel. 301 459 3366; fax 301 429 5746; www.nbnbooks.com

Australian agent/distributor: Pan Macmillan Australia,
Level 18, St Martins Tower, 31 Market St, Sydney, NSW 2000;
tel. 1300 135 113; fax 1300 135 103; customer.service@macmillan.com.au

New Zealand agent/distributor: David Bateman Ltd, 30 Tarndale Grove, Off Bush Road, Albany, Auckland;
tel. (09) 415 7664; fax (09) 415 8892

Publisher: Joanna Lorenz
Managing Editor: Linda Fraser
Senior Editor: Susannah Blake
Copy Editor: Rosie Hankin
Editorial Reader: Jonathon Marshall
Recipes: Brian Glover, Christine Ingram, Lucy Knox, Jane Milton, Jennie Shapter,
  Marlena Spieler, Kate Whiteman
Designer: Oakley Design Associates
Photographers: Martin Brigdale, Gus Filgate, David King, William Lingwood, Sam Stowell

Previously published as *Beat Asthma Through Diet*

10 9 8 7 6 5 4 3 2 1

NOTES

Bracketed terms are intended for American readers.

For all recipes, quantities are given in both metric and imperial measures and, where appropriate, measures
are also given in standard cups and spoons. Follow one set, but not a mixture, because they are not
interchangeable.

Standard spoon and cup measures are level.
1 tsp = 5ml, 1 tbsp = 15ml, 1 cup = 250ml/8fl oz

Australian standard tablespoons are 20ml. Australian readers should use 3 tsp in place of 1 tbsp for
measuring small quantities of gelatine, flour, salt, etc.

Medium (US large) eggs are used unless otherwise stated.

The diets and information in this book are not intended to replace advice from a qualified practitioner, doctor or
dietician. Always consult your health practitioner before adopting any of the suggestions
in this book.

contents

asthma, eczema and hayfever

AROUND THE WORLD – especially in the West – more and more people are suffering from asthma, eczema and hayfever, conditions that may be caused by intolerance or allergy to substances we eat, drink, touch or inhale. In the US it is thought that up to 15 million people have symptoms of asthma, and in the UK one in eight children and one in thirteen adults are affected. However, Australia tops the international league with one in three children having asthma symptoms.

ASTHMA SYMPTOMS

The symptoms of asthma vary from person to person and may be accompanied by extreme anxiety, sweating and increased pulse rate. You may not suffer from all these symptoms at any one time and their severity may vary at different times:

- A long-lasting cough, often worse at night or after exercise
- Wheezing (the whistling sound produced as air is expelled from the lungs) – this may be very quiet and sometimes can only be heard with the aid of a stethoscope
- Shortness of breath
- Difficulty breathing out
- Tightness of the chest

The following symptoms are likely to occur in a severe attack:

- Breathing becomes increasingly shallow and fast
- The lips and face may turn blue as oxygen levels in the blood diminish
- The skin may become pale and feel clammy

WARNING:

Severe asthma attacks can kill. If someone is suffering from a severe attack, call an ambulance immediately, then place the patient in the recovery position until medical attention arrives.

If you are prone to severe asthma attacks, make sure that you always keep your inhaler with you.

A MODERN PROBLEM

There is no simple answer as to why more people are suffering. Allergies are common in the developed world, but rare in countries without our industries, pollution and medicines. It could be that over thousands of years, the human body has developed the ability to defend itself against natural compounds, but we have fewer defences against the many new and artificial substances.

Above: *Air pollution in the developed world is thought to be one of the major contributing factors in causing asthma.*

Left: *In some parts of the world as many as one in three children suffer from asthma.*

ABOUT ASTHMA

If you – or perhaps a member of your family – are one the world's many asthma sufferers, you will know that the symptoms can vary from mild wheezing and coughing to a terrifying inability to breathe, which can be life threatening. For this reason it is vital to follow your doctor's recommendations at all times and – whatever else you may try in terms of self help – to keep any vital medications always at hand.

Technically, asthma is an inflammatory condition in which the muscles in the walls of your lungs' tiny airways go into spasm. At much the same time that the spasms occur, the linings of the airways swell up and thick mucus is produced. All this makes it difficult for you to get air in and out of your lungs. A variety of factors such as cold air, exercise, infections or common allergens including house dust mites and pollen may trigger an attack.

THE CAUSES AND SYMPTOMS OF ECZEMA

Like asthma, eczema is linked to allergies and shows up as patches of dry, scaly skin, which may crack, itch, become reddened, swell and/or weep. These are often located in the creases of joints around the body. Damaged skin is more open to infection so there may also be pimples or pus. Symptoms

can range from mildly irritating to almost unbearable, and may change according to the time of day or the season of the year. Sufferers of eczema also often find symptoms become worse when under pressure or suffering from emotional stress.

Above: *For sufferers of hayfever, late spring and early summer can prove to be a misery as they react to the grass and flower pollen in the air. Sneezing, a running nose and itchy, inflamed eyes are all common symptoms.*

URTICARIA

This skin condition, which often occurs in people with asthma and eczema, is also known as hives or nettlerash. It is usually, though not always, triggered by an allergic reaction to a particular food such as cow's milk, eggs, shellfish, strawberries or nuts, or to food additives such as the food colourant tartrazine.

Urticaria can also be caused by certain medicines such as aspirin and penicillin, or by insect stings, pollen and dander, which are small particles or scales of animal hair or feathers. For some people, stress or tension can make urticaria worse.

If you develop urticaria, white or yellow itchy lumps surrounded by a red area of inflammation develop on the skin. You may also suffer swelling – called angio-oedema – of the face, lips, eyelids, tongue or throat. This is often due to food allergy or intolerance and can come on within seconds of food entering the mouth.

Urticaria is usually an irritating but harmless condition. However, if you suffer an attack of angio-oedema and the swelling begins to spread to your throat, contact your doctor immediately as there is a slight risk of suffocation.

HAVING HAYFEVER

If you – or your child – has hayfever, you will know exactly how maddening this particular allergy can be. Just when the sun has come out and everyone else seems to be enjoying themselves outside in the fresh air, you can't stop sneezing, your nose is running and your eyes are red, weeping and itchy. You may also be wheezing, have shortness of breath and a dry throat.

Hayfever is an allergic reaction to air-borne pollen from grasses and flowers, and it can affect the nose, throat and eyes. The condition is seasonal, and occurs mainly in late spring and early summer, though the exact timing of when symptoms develop will depend on which type of specific pollen you are allergic to.

how food can cause allergy and intolerance

YOUR DIET can have an important part to play in allergies. A nutritious diet can help keep your immune system in tip-top condition, warding off the bugs that can trigger asthma and make hayfever and eczema worse. If your allergies are triggered by certain foods, you can try to find out what these are – and then avoid them. But, to understand how food triggers your symptoms, it helps to know about allergic responses.

IMMUNE SYSTEM OVERREACTION

Allergic reactions are rather like your body's response to any foreign substance – be they germs or splinters. Normally, your body responds with a range of defences, called antibodies, to fight off any invaders (antigens). Familiar signs of this fight in your body include swelling, redness and fever – all healthy indications that your immune system is at work.

If you are prone to allergies however, your immune system overdoes it, recognising usually harmless substances, such as pollen or foods, as enemies and attempting to fight them off. Once your body has mistaken these harmless substances for the enemy, it remembers what happened the last time and sets up a system for making the antibodies quickly, in case the invader returns.

It is this overreaction by the body's natural defence mechanisms to a foreign body that causes a range of symptoms anywhere in the body. As well as the symptoms of asthma, eczema and hayfever, allergy can cause other unpleasant reactions such as vomiting and diarrhoea, headaches and migraine, tiredness, wakefulness at night and irritability.

ANTIBODIES AT WORK

The main antibody that causes these allergic symptoms is immunoglobulin E (IgE). It becomes active chiefly in the blood, the mucous membranes of the nose, throat and mouth, and in the skin. When the enemy invader shows up in the body, IgE reacts with the antigen and sets off a release

of various chemicals. The best known of these chemicals is histamine, and it (together with other chemicals produced by cell tissue) causes the familiar, immediate symptoms of allergy, from itchy skin, running nose and sneezing, and itchy eyes to tiredness, headaches and irritability. Histamine is produced by the body whenever it is injured

Above: *Eating a balanced diet is essential for good health, but some common foods can also be the cause of allergies.*

or under attack from infection. It causes the blood vessels to increase in size so that blood can quickly get to damaged tissue in order to repair it.

ANAPHYLACTIC SHOCK

This massive allergic reaction is a rare but potentially life-threatening event during which the blood vessels suddenly swell, causing a dramatic drop in blood pressure. This in turn leads to a lack of oxygen in the brain. Without sufficient oxygen, the brain cannot control blood pressure, which can cause it to fall even further. Once into this downward spiral, your body cannot recover of its own accord.

As blood pressure continues to fall the sufferer may become drowsy and confused, and might finally lose consciousness.

Anaphylaxsis can be triggered by a variety of allergens, the most common of which are foods (especially peanuts, some other nuts, eggs, cow's milk and products made from it, and shellfish); certain drugs such as penicillin; the venom of stinging insects such as bees, wasps and hornets; latex and paint.

The symptoms – which may appear very suddenly and without any warning – can include:
- Sweating, faintness and nausea
- Panting and rapid pulse rate
- Pale, cold, clammy skin
- Hives may appear on the skin

If you are with someone who is going into anaphylactic shock, call an ambulance immediately. Meanwhile lie them down – on their side if already unconscious – wrap them in a coat or blanket and do not give them anything to eat or drink.

If you know that you or your child is at risk of anaphylaxis, your doctor will prescribe medication for use in the event of an allergic reaction. This may include a pre-loaded injection of adrenaline (epinephrine), and antihistamines and hydrocortisone may also be given.

Above: *Although milk is considered healthy and nutritious, particularly for children, it can also be the cause of food allergy and intolerance in others.*

ALLERGY AND INTOLERANCE: TELLING THE DIFFERENCE

The dividing line between allergy and intolerance is rather blurred, so much so that intolerance is sometimes referred to as "pseudo-allergy". Intolerance can be difficult to "prove" and so traditionally the medical profession has been sceptical of its existence, and therefore its treatment. Intolerance, like allergy, occurs when the body's immune system overreacts to foreign substances, but the process is much slower and the symptoms are not so obvious.

With allergy, the response is usually quick and noticeable almost immediately – or at least within 72 hours. Intolerance, on the other hand, tends to reveal itself much more slowly. If a person is allergic to cats, for instance, you will probably be able to tell there is a cat in the room (or even that a cat has been in the room) because the person's eyes and nose will start to run within just a few minutes. In contrast, an intolerance to a commonly eaten food such as wheat can take

months or even years to develop. Because of this very slow response, it is often much more difficult to work out what is causing the symptoms of intolerance than it is to discover the cause of an allergic reaction.

The mechanism of intolerance may be different from that of allergy, too. During an allergic reaction, the body fights an invader and produces the chemical histamine. With intolerance, the body does not necessarily produce a histamine reaction.

When a person has an intolerance to a substance, it may be an ingredient of food – such as gluten in cereals, proteins in cheese or fish, or caffeine in coffee, tea, cola drinks and chocolate – which directly harms or irritates the body. Another reason for intolerance may be that a person lacks the physical ability to cope with certain foods. For example, people who have an intolerance to dairy products usually have a shortage of the enzyme lactase. Without this enzyme, the lactose in dairy products cannot be digested properly.

SYMPTOMS OF INTOLERANCE

One complication of identifying intolerance is that some of the common symptoms of intolerance overlap with those of certain allergies, for instance, tiredness, migraine, nausea and vomiting. Symptoms of intolerance include:
- Aching muscles
- Mouth ulcers
- Water retention
- Gastric and duodenal ulcers
- Wind and bloating, IBS (irritable bowel syndrome) and constipation
- Rheumatoid arthritis
- Anxiety and depression
- Hyperactivity in children and ADD (attention deficit disorder)

why people suffer from allergies

THE WHOLE SUBJECT of allergy and intolerance is a contentious one – especially when it comes to identifying causes. This is partly because we don't know all the answers to how and why allergies and intolerances occur, and partly because health practitioners can take very different approaches in treatment.

HEREDITY

Is it in your genes? Heredity seems to play a part in who gets allergies, although these can show up in different forms within the same family. For instance, if one of your parents suffers from hayfever, you may get asthma and your child might develop eczema.

Research shows that if one of your parents has an allergy, you have a 20–30 per cent chance of developing one. If both your parents have allergies, you have a 40–60 per cent chance of having one. If both your parents have the same allergy, you have a 70 per cent chance of developing that allergy. However, a third of children with allergies are born to parents who aren't aware of any allergic symptoms in themselves.

Below: *Allergies often run in families yet, in over one third of these, sufferers develop symptoms their parents didn't have.*

OTHER FAMILY INFLUENCES

The family influence is more than genetics. Some recent studies into childhood illnesses suggest that the more people are exposed to infections, the less likely they are to develop allergies. The same may be true for dust and dirt. There is evidence that children with older siblings – and who are introduced that way to more infections – suffer less from allergy than first born children.

While allergies and intolerances seem to run in families, children will inherit only a tendency to allergy. Whether or not a full-blown allergy develops depends very much on their diet and environment, not only in the sensitive weeks and months after birth, but also before birth while the child is still in the womb. To help reduce the chances of your child developing allergic conditions, follow the guidelines given in the advice box on early preventive measures.

OUR POLLUTED ENVIRONMENT

There is no definitive proof, but the emerging consensus is that environmental pollution even in moderation is a significant trigger for common allergies like asthma. Toxins from the air could be compromising our immunity as well as irritating our airways.

Not only the air we breathe, but also our water and our food often contain chemicals, such as pesticides, additives and artificial flavourings. We also come into regular contact with many other toxins including heavy metals from petrol fumes, mercury in some tooth fillings, and chemicals in cosmetics and detergents.

Inside the home

Protected by insulation and double glazing, our modern homes may be warm and dry but they are poorly ventilated and they trap:

- Fumes given off by solvent-based paints, varnishes, cleaning fluids and glues
- Formaldehyde from soft furnishings
- Nitrogen oxide and carbon monoxide from gas appliances
- A range of pollutants in cigarette smoke

Outside the home

We talk about getting a "breath of fresh air", but consider the following:

- Exhaust fumes and heavy industry mean we are ingesting about 1000 times as much lead as our prehistoric ancestors
- Ozone, a chemical cocktail containing hydrocarbons and nitrogen oxides, is beginning to pose a major health problem in some cities. This gas is thought to be responsible for causing increased asthma attacks, headaches, eye irritation, coughs and other respiratory problems
- Pollen in the air can bring on an allergic response in hayfever sufferers and an asthma attack in allergic asthmatics

EARLY PREVENTIVE MEASURES

- Pregnant women should avoid eating peanuts or any foods that contain peanuts. Babies exposed to peanuts while still in the womb may be more likely to develop this allergy
- Breastfeeding mothers should also avoid eating peanuts. Check that peanut oil (sometimes labelled arachis oil or groundnut oil) is not an ingredient of nipple or skin cream
- Breastfeed your baby for at least six months (longer if possible) and give your baby nothing but breastmilk for the first four to six months. Breastfeeding affords the best possible protection against all sorts of illnesses, including allergy
- Avoid the common allergy-causing foods while you are breastfeeding, as whatever you eat or drink finds its way into breast milk
- If there is a history of allergy in your family, do not give your child peanuts to eat until he or she is about five years old. Meanwhile, avoid using any commercial infant creams that contain peanut oil
- Introduce solids slowly, in small quantities and one at a time. Avoid wheat, rye, barley, fish, soya, citrus fruits and sesame seeds until your baby is at least six months old
- If allergies run in your family, avoid cow's milk products until your child is one year old

INSIDE YOUR BODY

Antibiotics and vaccines

The relatively recent worldwide increase in allergies appears to coincide both with the increased use of antibiotics and the administration of childhood vaccinations. Many complementary practitioners believe that the vaccination of children actually reduces their body's need to activate an immune response early in life and that this may increase allergic tendencies.

Stress

We can also be made more susceptible to allergies by stress. While we may not experience more stress than our ancestors, our modern sedentary way of life causes stress to build up inside us. Instead of running or fighting when faced with stress – as nature intended – we are more often than not stuck behind a desk or the wheel of a car. Yet stress causes the release of two hormones: adrenaline (epinephrine) and cortisol (or hydrocortisone). Adrenaline speeds up the body, uses up nutrients and can lead to deficiencies in vitamin B_6 (pyridoxine), amino acids and zinc. All these changes can lead to a weakening of the immune system.

Cortisol, known as the body's natural steroid, is an immune suppressant. You might think that suppressing the immune response would be no bad thing when dealing with allergies or intolerances but, unfortunately, when cortisol diminishes the body goes into rebound, creating an even stronger inflammatory response.

Foods

There is some evidence that the symptoms of asthma, eczema and hayfever may be triggered by a particular food. Allergic reaction to certain foods is often immediate and severe, with vomiting, rashes, eczema, asthma, or even anaphylactic shock. Food intolerance produces a less acute and much slower reaction, and is often triggered by foods that are eaten frequently – and which the sufferer craves.

Left: *It is best for pregnant women to avoid any foods or products containing peanuts.*

Foods that may trigger asthma and eczema in some people include cow's milk and other dairy products, alcohol, yeasts (and foods that may contain yeasts, such as dried fruit) and seafood.

Leaky gut syndrome

Another possible cause of food intolerance is leaky gut syndrome. Your small intestine is a kind of sieve that should allow only the breakdown products of digestion into your bloodstream (for instance amino acids and peptides, broken down from proteins). Larger particles of protein, carbohydrate and fat are usually sieved out so that they don't get into the blood. This is because your body may react to these larger particles as the enemy, and trigger an attack response from your immune system.

However, in leaky gut syndrome, this sieve mechanism breaks down and fails to work so that foods that have not been digested fully are absorbed into the bloodstream. This syndrome may have a number of causes, ranging from foods that inflame the bowels to certain drugs and yeasts that can actually make tiny holes in the walls of the gut.

Below: *Take time to relax, as a build up of stress can make you susceptible to allergies.*

finding the common food triggers

IT CAN BE A LONG and complicated process to find out which foods, amongst other things, are setting off your allergic reactions. However, it is often possible to identify your personal food culprits and find foods to alleviate your symptoms. There is a wide range of elimination diets to try, some more arduous than others. Remember that children, in particular, should maintain a balanced diet, so consult a nutritionist first.

FOOD ELIMINATION DIETS
The "food group" exclusion diet

Allergies and food intolerance can be caused by a specific group of foods, such as dairy products, grains or citrus fruits. To find out if one of these groups of foods is causing your allergic reactions, pick one group and cut out foods belonging to it. For example, if the group is grain, eliminate wheat, rice, rye, corn, millet etc. If the group is dairy, then eliminate all cow's milk products. Other food groups are animal protein (meat, fish, eggs, cheese) and vegetable protein (wholegrain cereals, lentils, beans, tofu, soya).

Keep up this diet for six weeks. If you see no improvement, you are looking in the wrong direction. If you do see an improvement, carry on for three months before trying to reintroduce the foods.

The "favourite foods" exclusion diet

This diet works on the principle that an allergic response can often develop to the foods you eat most.

Cut out your five favourite foods, plus the five foods that you eat most (these are quite likely to overlap), from your diet for a minimum period of at least six weeks.

If you see no improvement, these foods are unlikely to be the source of the problem. If you do see an improvement, keep up the diet for three months, then reintroduce foods you dropped from your diet one at a time to see if your body reacts.

If you respond allergically to the reintroduced food, keep off it for another six weeks then try again. If you still respond allergically, keep off the food for about three months before you try again.

Above: *Red wine, bread, cheese, chocolate and milk are all commonly eaten foods that can cause allergic responses.*

The "lamb and pears" diet

Exclude all foods except lamb and pears from your diet for seven to ten days. Very few people have an allergic response to lamb or pears. If you wish, substitute two other foods that you don't normally eat, for instance mackerel and courgettes (zucchini). Gradually reintroduce other foods to your diet and note your response.

The "Stone Age" diet

A number of scientists believe that we took a wrong turn in our diets about 10,000 years ago when we ceased to be hunter-gatherers and began to rely on agriculture.

This diet avoids all "recent" foods such as cereals, dairy produce, sugar, food additives, coffee, tea and alcohol. Instead, you follow a restricted diet of fresh meat, fish, fruit, vegetables and nuts.

Below: *Grains such as corn, wheat and rice may cause allergic reactions. You need to eliminate them from your diet to find out if they are the cause of your symptoms.*

Below: *Citrus fruits are one of the common triggers for allergies and intolerance. Try cutting out this group of foods to see if it makes an improvement to your condition.*

Above: *If you feel that you need to take drastic action to find out which foods are triggering your symptoms, try eating only lamb and pears for a week as very few people are allergic to these two foods.*

The rotation diet

If you are mildly allergic or intolerant towards different foods, achieving a healthy balanced diet can be difficult. By eating each of these foods in rotation, only once every four days (or longer), you can maintain a healthy diet and reduce your allergic response.

DIAGNOSTIC TESTS

If you don't want to try an elimination diet – or if this hasn't worked – there are a number of diagnostic tests that may be helpful in identifying your triggers:

Skin tests

Patch testing This is often used to detect the allergens responsible for eczema. Tiny patches saturated in a number of different substances – from plant extracts to solvents – are stuck to the skin on your back and left for two to three days. When the patches are removed, areas of redness or swelling indicate allergy.

The "pin prick" test In this test, small or dilute amounts of suspected allergens are pinpricked under the skin. If the person is allergic, their skin will begin to itch and a raised red weal will develop. The bigger the weal, the more allergic they are.

Blood tests

ELISA (enzyme-linked immunosorbent assay) and RAST (radioallergosorbent) These tests are used to measure the amount of IgE produced in the blood by allergic reactions. Only a small sample of blood is taken for testing.

FACT (food allergy cellular test) This is useful in complex cases where many allergens may be involved as it tests not only for IgE but also for IgG4 (an immunoglobulin that is produced against certain foods and other allergens) and leukotrienes (chemicals that are released by white blood cells that have recognized an invader).

ALCAT (antigen allergy cellular test) This test is designed to measure the activity of white blood cells.

OTHER TESTS

Bio-resonance testing This is based on the Eastern belief that there are energy channels – or meridians – throughout the body. Bio-resonance machines are specialized computers that send small electric currents around your body to measure your energy field and detect abnormalities. Used by complementary practitioners to indicate allergens, the machine may also be used to "switch off" the allergic response.

Gut permeability test This test may be suggested by a complementary practitioner if leaky gut syndrome is suspected. You will be given a drink containing many different sized molecules. Your urine is then collected over a period of about six hours and the size of the molecules present in the urine are measured. If there are very large molecules present – or if there are too many of one particular kind of molecule getting through the gut wall – then leaky gut syndrome can be confirmed.

Kinesiology A small quantity of the suspect allergen is placed on your abdomen. The kinesiologist then pushes against your arm (usually) to test for muscle weakness. This is believed to show whether a substance has a negative effect on you. (This test has not been proven but some people find that it can be very effective.)

Below: *Fresh vegetables, fish and fruit are the basis of the "Stone Age" diet.*

how to alleviate your symptoms

IF YOU OR YOUR CHILD have asthma, eczema or hayfever, there are many things you can do to make life better. Identifying and avoiding potential allergens in your diet is important, but there are many more things that you can do to reduce your exposure to other allergens.

Above: If you have allergy-related asthma or eczema, improving your diet by eating locally produced, organic vegetables may help to alleviate your symptoms.

EAT LOCAL FOODS IN SEASON

If our modern diet – rich in imported exotic fruits and vegetables – is the cause of many allergy-related problems, it makes sense to return to a more natural diet that relies on locally grown produce, eaten in season.

Include at least five portions of fruit and vegetables a day. Eat tomatoes, lettuce and other salad vegetables – preferably organic – in the summer when they are home-produced.

KEEP HEALTHY AND HAPPY

Whatever your allergy, the symptoms are likely to be less severe if you are in good health. A strong immune system staves off infections – such as colds and flu – which can trigger asthma attacks in some people. Follow these golden rules:

- Sleep well. Most adults need eight hours, children far more. Drink chamomile tea at bedtime.
- Get plenty of exercise. Even 20 minutes a day can improve your health. Holistic forms of exercise such as yoga and t'ai chi can help you keep fit physically, mentally and emotionally.
- Have a good breakfast. Organic porridge provides instant energy and also slow-release energy to keep you going. Some complementary practitioners believe unrefined oats also have a calming effect on your system, which may benefit your heart and encourage healthy circulation.
- Avoid excessive alcohol consumption. This can cause serious depression, lower immunity to infections, raise blood pressure and disrupt sleep.
- Don't smoke. Cigarettes are full of poisons that can do your body nothing but harm – let alone the implications smoking has for asthma.
- Drink up to eight glasses of water a day if you can. This helps to dilute any allergens in your system and may reduce the immune over-response.
- Enjoy yourself. Go out, see friends and have a good time.

Above: Lavender oil is one of the many aromatic essential oils that can be used to help you relax or sleep.

AROMATHERAPY

Essential oils have been used for thousands of years for healing and promoting a general feeling of relaxation and wellbeing. Use aromatic lavender oil in your bath or put a few drops on your pillow at bedtime to help you to sleep. If you are pregnant or breastfeeding, consult your doctor before using any essential oils.

RELAXATION IS IMPORTANT

There are many different ways to relax – from listening to music to lying in a flotation tank. Find one that is right for you and make a regular habit of it. Stress can increase and prolong the symptoms of allergy, and can trigger attacks of asthma and eczema so try to counteract it by making time to relax.

Left: A glass of chamomile tea before bedtime will help you sleep better, which in turn will keep you healthy and well.

MEDITATION

Take 20 minutes out of your day to meditate and switch off. Find somewhere comfortable and warm to sit or lie down (you may prefer to meditate in the dark), then slowly breathe in through your nose and out through your mouth. Count each out breath and once you reach ten, start again from one. Repeat this cycle of ten breaths over and over again. Then count the in breaths in cycles of ten. After a while, stop counting and just watch the breath, concentrating on its flow. Then focus your attention on the point at which each breath first enters your body and be aware of how it feels. With practice, you will be able to exclude all distracting thoughts, feelings and worries— and feel very relaxed indeed.

HOW TO AVOID ALLERGENS

Another crucial aspect of self-help for people with allergies such as asthma, eczema and hayfever is avoiding whatever makes them worse. Here are some ideas on dealing with common culprits.

Dust mite faeces

These are in every home and are one of the main causes of asthma. Reduce them by taking the following measures:

- Remove curtains, carpets and as many other soft furnishings as you can from your home.
- Cover mattresses, pillows and duvets (filled with man-made fibres) with special barrier covers.
- To kill dust mites, wash all bedding regularly at above 55°C (131°F)
- Vacuum floors and soft furnishings every day.
- Dust mites love warm, moist conditions, so keep your home cool, dry and well aired. Use an extractor fan when bathing or cooking, and always try to dry laundry outdoors.
- Soft toys are dust mite havens, so wrap them in a plastic bag and put them in the freezer for a couple of hours. The low temperature will kill any dust mites.

Above: *Practising a relaxation technique such as meditation can help to alleviate the symptoms of eczema and asthma.*

Pollen and mould spores

These are the big culprits in hayfever. Use the information and tips below to help lessen your symptoms:

- If your hayfever symptoms are at their worst in late spring and early summer, grass pollen is likely to be the culprit.
- The grass pollen count varies throughout the day and tends to be highest in late afternoon and early evening, especially in cities. A high count can persist through the night.
- Hayfever sufferers often notice an increase in their symptoms before a thunder storm and as heavy rain begins.
- The pollen count tends to be lowest on dull, damp days.
- Keep your windows – especially in the bedroom – closed during the day. You can open the bedroom window again when you go to bed. Windy weather can blow grass and tree pollens many miles – and through your open windows.
- Try to keep your car windows closed when driving.
- Stay indoors, if possible, with the windows closed on high pollen count days.

- Wear sunglasses when the pollen count is high and bathe your eyes to remove pollen.
- Avoid hanging clothes to dry in the garden on high pollen count days as they will collect pollen.
- If you are allergic to tree pollens avoid areas of uncut, flowering grass, or flowering woodland.
- If you are allergic to mould spores, keep away from woodland in the autumn.
- Change your clothes and shower when you come indoors.
- Pets can collect pollen on their fur as they move through flowering grass. Ask a non-hayfever sufferer to brush them before they come inside.
- Get someone else to mow the lawn.
- Opt for a low allergy garden. Avoid grasses, hedges, trees, mould-producing mulches and heavily scented pollinated flowers. Go for paved or gravelled areas with pot plants and ground-cover plants (to cut down on pollen-producing weeds).

EASING ECZEMA

Eczema – and other allergy – sufferers are likely to benefit from taking the following steps:

- Wear natural fabrics such as cotton or linen that allow your skin to keep dry, cool and yeast free.
- Use old-fashioned cleaning methods – soap and water, soda crystals, damp dusting – rather than modern chemical-based cleaning products.
- Avoid wearing bright or dark-coloured clothing because deep dyes may cause allergic rashes on sensitive skin.
- Make your garden organic, especially if you grow fruit and vegetables. This will help to reduce your "chemical load".
- Avoid using solvent-based paints, varnishes and other DIY products, especially in bedrooms or if you are pregnant.

using modern medical treatments

IF YOU SUFFER FROM ALLERGIES, you may well be very grateful for any medication your doctor has prescribed. For people with asthma in particular, drugs can be a life-saver. However, orthodox medical treatments for allergies are not cures; they are designed to suppress the symptoms and relieve discomfort. The underlying condition will not be eliminated, but it should be controlled.

DRUG TREATMENTS FOR ASTHMA

In orthodox medicine, there are two basic kinds of treatment for asthma. The first type, known as "relievers" or bronchodilators, work by relaxing the muscles around the airways when they constrict. Relievers can be taken as a rescue when you experience symptoms, or when you expect symptoms to appear.

This type of medication is usually taken from an inhaler, and may include the drugs salbutamol and tarbutaline. Reliever drugs act in a similar manner to adrenaline (epinephrine), the substance your body naturally produces to increase your heart rate or to open your airways.

The second type of medication given to asthma sufferers is known as "preventers". These drugs are designed to treat any inflammation of the airways and thus stop asthma symptoms from developing. Because they are designed to suppress the symptoms not cure the condition, preventers have to be used regularly to be effective. Non-steroidal drugs such as sodium cromoglycate, are often prescribed for children. For adults, inhaled steroid drugs (such as beclomethasone or budesonide) are more often prescribed.

Asthma sufferers may need extra medication at times, particularly if they react badly to stress or environmental factors such as cold air or dust mites.

CREAMS AND DRUG TREATMENTS FOR ECZEMA

Eczema is common in families with a history of allergies, including asthma and hayfever. Orthodox treatment involves treating the symptoms usually with topical steroid creams in combination with soothing lotions. Topical steroids work by controlling and damping down inflammation in the skin. They alleviate the itching and remove the urge to scratch the affected area, which allows the skin to heal.

Some corticosteroid medication (such as prednisolone and prednisone) may be given orally, however, there is a risk of side effects with these drugs.

Topical steroids can be very effective in the short term. But the more they are used, the less effective they can become – and the side-effects may become unacceptable. Old-fashioned pastes and ointments, based on coal tar, can also be effective in treating eczema, although many people find that the smell and the messiness of these preparations is unacceptable.

Occasionally, doctors will also prescribe a course of antibiotics if the skin becomes infected. Finally, ultraviolet light (UVA) treatment used in combination with the drug psoralen is known as PUVA. This treatment can sometimes be effective for long-term eczema sufferers.

Eczema sufferers will be aware of the changing seasons and the need for increased medication at some times of the year.

Left: *A young boy is taught to use an inhaler to improve his breathing during an asthma attack. By pumping the drug into a bottle, the sufferer is able to inhale the dosage normally.*

PROS AND CONS OF CONVENTIONAL TREATMENTS

Pros:

- Are life-saving in extreme cases such as asthma or anaphylactic shock
- Give immediate, or very quick, relief of symptoms
- May stop symptoms developing
- Allow allergy sufferers to manage their own condition with as little change to their lifestyle as possible
- Adverse reactions to conventional drug treatments are rare

Cons:

- May have side-effects, such as drowsiness or loss of appetite
- Alleviate the symptoms, but do not address the underlying causes of the allergy
- Often necessitate increasing doses of medication – the more the treatment is used the less effective it is likely to become
- The use of steroid drugs over a long period of time may cause a range of problems, which is of particular concern when treating young children

DRUG TREATMENTS FOR HAYFEVER

The best way to treat an allergy is to avoid the substance causing the allergic reaction but this can be difficult in the case of air-borne pollen. Treatment for hayfever depends very much on your doctor. Some practitioners prefer one-dose antihistamine tablets, which have no sedative side effects, but act on the whole body. Others prefer local, targeted treatments, including nasal corticosteroids and nasal antihistamines (for a very blocked nose) or eye drops containing antihistamine and decongestant (for very puffy eyes). Preventive drops are made from sodium cromoglycate, which most doctors consider safe.

Desensitizing injections may also be considered by your doctor if your hayfever is very severe. However these have to be taken all year round – not just when the symptoms are unbearable – and entail regular visits to the hospital or clinic. Now that the trigger for hayfever has been identified as part of a protein called profilin, a new treatment for the condition may eventually be forthcoming.

Depending on the time of year, hayfever suffers will need varying levels of medication during different seasons.

Below: *There are specially designed inhalers for asthmatic babies.*

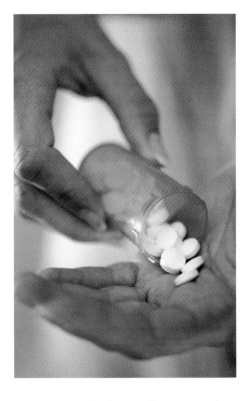

Above: *Many hayfever sufferers control their symptoms with antihistamine tablets, which are convenient and can greatly improve their allergic response.*

Below: *Hayfever sufferers often find soothing eye drops can alleviate the discomfort of itchy, puffy eyes caused by their allergic reaction to pollen.*

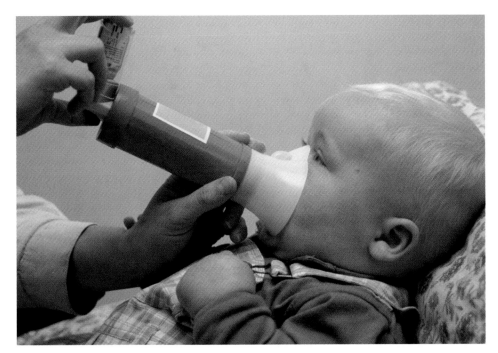

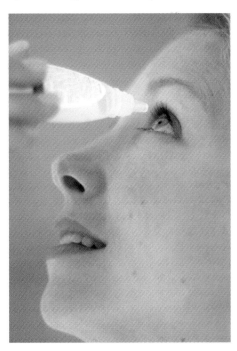

complementary treatments

ALL OVER THE WESTERN WORLD, people are turning increasingly to complementary therapies. This does not necessarily mean giving up conventional medicines and many practitioners would urge you to adopt an "integrated" approach. An increasing number of doctors now accept that complementary therapies can help with asthma, eczema and hayfever. However, do try to discuss the therapy you are considering with your doctor before beginning treatment.

SPOILT FOR CHOICE

One of the problems often faced by people who want to try a complementary therapy is that there are so many of them, all apparently using different methods. So how do you decide which therapy suits you best? Here is a brief outline of some of the therapies that are most effective in treating asthma, eczema and hayfever.

PROS AND CONS OF COMPLEMENTARY TREATMENTS

Pros:

- Complementary therapies are holistic, addressing not just your symptoms but every aspect of your health – physical, mental, emotional and spiritual
- You may find a therapy that eliminates the cause of your allergy
- There are rarely any side effects with complementary treatment

Cons:

- Complementary therapy works to restore the body's natural balance – it is not a quick fix
- It may be weeks or months before benefits become evident
- Treatments work most effectively as part of a healthy lifestyle that includes exercise and balanced diet
- They can be expensive
- There may not be a qualified practitioner in your area

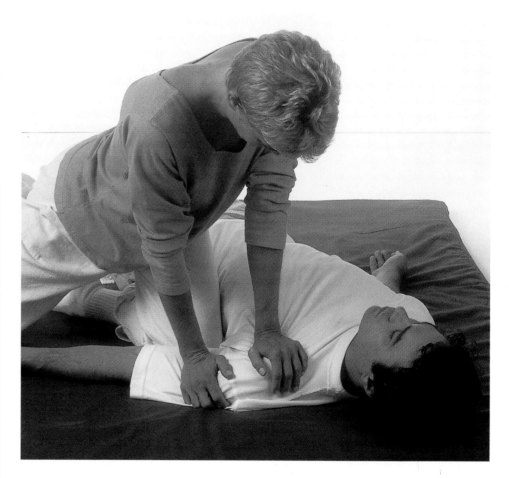

HOMEOPATHY

The principle of this complementary healing system is to "treat like with like". Patients are treated with tiny doses of substances that would cause the symptoms of their illness in a healthy person. Homeopaths believe this will stimulate your body's own healing process, as opposed to treating symptoms alone, which may bring only temporary relief. Homeopathic practice involves a full assessment of your physical and mental health,

Above: *Some people find that alternative therapies such as Shiatsu help to improve their respiratory function by promoting relaxation and deeper breathing.*

and may also include specific allergy or intolerance testing. Once you have established any substances or foods that may trigger your allergy, your practitioner will discuss further treatment, from desensitization to treatment with established homeopathic remedies.

Above: *Raw fruits and vegetables in juice form are often prescribed by naturopaths to boost the immune system.*

NATUROPATHY

Modern naturopathy seeks to treat and avert disease by bolstering the body's own defence systems, primarily through a healthy diet and sensible lifestyle. Following a detailed consultation, your naturopath will advise on diet, exercise and other treatment for your condition. Naturopaths regard a healthy diet – based on raw, organic food – as the best form of medicine. This is often combined with other treatments to stimulate your body's vital force, rather than to suppress your symptoms. Raw fruits and vegetables in juice form are also often prescribed.

NUTRITIONAL THERAPY

The use of food, vitamin, mineral and other supplements to cure and prevent disease is an increasingly scientific and complex field. Research shows that a heavily processed "junk food" diet is linked to asthma – as well as many other health problems.

Treatment begins with a detailed questionnaire about your medical history, symptoms, diet and lifestyle. The practitioner may also undertake a number of tests to pinpoint any dietary problems, allergies or intolerances. Treatment programmes consist of nutritional advice, a short-term diet tailored to suit your condition and a course of supplements that may include vitamins, minerals or herbs.

ACUPUNCTURE

One of the best known and most respected complementary therapies, acupuncture is part of a comprehensive system of traditional Chinese medicine dating back thousands of years. Acupuncture involves using very fine needles that are inserted at strategic points (acupoints) on the body to stimulate the vital flow of energy and correct imbalances which may be causing symptoms.

Following very careful observation and questioning, your practitioner will seek to restore balance and harmony through meridians in your body. You may feel a slight pinprick as the needle is inserted, and a sensation of tingling or numbness. Initially the needles are left in for only six to ten minutes, building to 20 to 25 minutes in later sessions. For those who find the prospect of needles too alarming, there are other forms of therapy related to acupuncture, sometimes known as "acupuncture without needles", which include Shiatsu massage, acupressure and laser and ultrasound acupuncture. These therapies are based on the same principles as acupuncture, stimulating key points to balance your energies.

Above: *Complementary therapists will recommend avoiding heavily processed and "junk" foods and opting for fresh, healthy, nutritious foods.*

Above: *Yoga can be used to reduce stress and improve breathing technique.*

BREATHING TREATMENTS

Many Eastern philosophies of health regard breathing as the central factor in staying well. Of the breathing techniques currently offered by complementary practitioners, the best known is remedial yoga. Yoga breathing, in particular, has the benefit of moving blocked energy in the body. Yoga breathing can also be valuable in treating allergic conditions, because it helps reduce the effects of stress.

Other, more recent, breathing treatments that are beneficial to health include:

- Oxygenesis: an easy-to-learn technique, developed in California, which enables individuals to learn the ideal breathing pattern for themselves.
- The Buteyko Method: developed by Dr Konstantin Buteyko, this therapy is based on the theory that many illnesses – including asthma and allergies – are caused by overbreathing. Practitioners claim the Buteyko Method can rapidly "cure" asthma and allergies with special breathing exercises.

healing through diet

CAN THE "WRONG" FOODS TRIGGER asthma, make eczema worse, or aggravate hayfever? Can the "right" foods improve general health and these conditions in particular? By and large the medical experts say "no", although a balanced diet is always recommended. Yet sufferers often disagree. Many people say that by identifying "culprit" ingredients and eating beneficial foods, they have managed to control their condition.

Above: *Onions are one of many foods that can reduce allergy symptoms – they are particularly helpful for asthma sufferers.*

FOOD CULPRITS AND HELPERS

While the experts continue to argue about cause and effect, it is well established that in some people, certain foods cause typical allergic reactions such as wheezing, nausea, hives, bloating, diarrhoea or vomiting. Food allergies affect about one in 50 people in the West, but babies, because their digestive and immune systems are not yet mature, are more susceptible – although many grow out of them in time.

Most of those who do suffer in this way are only allergic to one, or a limited number of foods, commonly cow's milk, eggs, wheat, soya, nuts, fish and shellfish. (Nut allergies are the commonest cause of anaphylaxsis.) Food allergies often show up as hives (urticaria), while eczema is often an allergic reaction to wheat, milk or eggs.

So if you suspect you have a food allergy, or that certain foods are making your symptoms worse, ask to see an allergy specialist who can give you an accurate diagnosis of the foods that may be causing you problems. (Remember that DIY dietary restrictions can be harmful – especially for children – so seek the advice of a qualified dietician or nutritionist). Once you have identified a food culprit, get into the habit of reading labels on food packages to be sure that you are avoiding your triggers. Unfortunately, allergy is so complex that it is unlikely that foods will be your only triggers – so don't stop taking prescribed medication.

ATHSMA FOOD CULPRITS

- Dairy products
- Eggs
- Fish and shellfish
- Nuts, especially peanuts
- Yeast (and products containing yeast, such as dried fruits, wine and beer)

Food additives such as monosodium glutamate (flavour enhancer), aspartame (sweetener), tartrazine E102 (food colourant), and the preservatives E210–E227 can act as irritants (rather than allergens) to asthma suffers.

ASTHMA FOOD HELPERS

- A good diet protects against colds and viruses that can trigger asthma
- Eat plenty of fresh fruit and vegetables
- Onions – which have anti-inflammatory properties – are likely to be good for those with asthma; try to eat one a day
- Vitamin C, bromelain and quercetin are often recommended by naturopaths for their anti-inflammatory properties

ECZEMA FOOD CULPRITS

- Wheat
- Cow's milk
- Eggs
- Artificial colourants

ECZEMA FOOD HELPERS

- Supplements of vitamin B, zinc, essential fatty acids and evening primrose oil can improve skin quality.

HAYFEVER

Some nutritionists suggest altering your diet a few weeks before your particular hayfever season begins. For instance, if you are allergic to grass pollen, avoid foods that are species of grass, such as wheat-based foods (bread, pasta, cakes and biscuits) and other gluten grains (rye, barley, and oats). Start

Below: *Fresh fruits such as kiwis and blackcurrants are rich in vitamin C and will help to relieve the symptoms of asthma.*

four weeks before your symptoms usually appear and continue throughout that pollen season. Use other starches – such as potatoes, beans and gram flour (which is made from chick-peas) – instead.

On the same plant family principle, if you are allergic to birch pollen, you may well be also allergic to apples and some other fruits (including peaches, apricots and nectarines).

Some nutritionists argue it can help to avoid dairy products during the summer

Below: *Wine and ripe cheeses are thought to exacerbate the symptoms of asthma, eczema and hayfever.*

Left: *Bread and pasta made with wheat, eggs, and fruit drinks that contain food colouring are thought to trigger excema in some people.*

(this may work for those with asthma, too) because these foods can make inflammation worse. Live yogurt can be an exception.

Nettle leaf tea, reishi mushrooms and eyebright are often used as anti-hayfever herbs. The homeopathic hayfever remedy, Pollenna, can also help.

ADVICE FOR ASTHMA, ECZEMA AND HAYFEVER SUFFERERS

- All of these conditions have been linked to a deficiency of "good fats", so a supplement of GLA may help
- Avoid histamine-loaded foods such as wine, beer, ripe cheeses, salami, pickled food, mackerel and tuna. Vitamin C and the supplement quercetin can help to eliminate histamines
- Drink plenty of fresh water
- Avoid salt
- Eat plenty of fresh fruit and vegetables
- Vitamin and minerals supplements which may be useful include vitamin B complex, vitamin C, zinc and magnesium

Below: *If you suffer from hayfever, you may find that a cup of nettle leaf tea will alleviate the symptoms.*

HELPING YOUR CHILD TO LIVE WITH ASTHMA, ECZEMA OR HAYFEVER

- Food elimination diets are tricky for children because common culprits like milk have essential nutrients. In addition, most babies with asthma don't have food triggers: viruses and cigarette smoke are the common culprits. However, if there is a strong family history of food allergy in your family, if your baby has both eczema and asthma, and symptoms showed up when you introduced a particular weaning food, discuss this with your doctor. It may be wise to try removing that food
- Soya milk may not be a useful alternative to cow's milk; children fed on soya milk instead of dairy milk are just as likely to develop asthma
- Breastfeeding mothers need to avoid foods to which they are allergic – and to avoid creams and lotions that may contain peanut oil (such as cracked nipple creams)
- When weaning, introduce foods and drinks (avoiding fizzy drinks) one at a time, and watch for allergic symptoms
- Avoid eggs and cow's milk until babies are one year old, and, if there is a family history of allergy to fish, nuts, peanuts or wheat flour, avoid these, too
- Rotate foods: allergies may develop from eating the same foods daily
- Don't give children peanuts until they are five years old
- Encourage your child to eat more fruit and vegetables. Try making fresh fruit salads. Serve sticks of vegetables such as carrot, red pepper and cucumber. Make easy-to-eat soups from puréed vegetables and pulses. Create thick smoothies using fresh fruits, and use both fruits and vegetables to make delicious drinks. Add grated vegetables such as carrots and courgettes (zucchini) to pasta sauces. Serve diluted fruit juices rather than drinks like orange squash or lemonade

appetizers
and soups

With a wide range of different recipes to try, dishes to help beat asthma, eczema or hayfever certainly don't have to be boring. All the recipes in this chapter are ideal to start a meal or, to eat as a light lunch, simply serve with crusty bread or crackers. Take your pick from dips, such as spicy pumpkin to boost the immune system or guacamole to relieve congestion. Or opt for a bowl of nourishing soup – roasted garlic and squash soup with tomato salsa is full of vitamin C to help fight histamines and spicy black-eyed bean soup is a good source of B vitamins, which can help improve the skin.

smoky aubergine and pepper salad

THIS WONDERFULLY AROMATIC SALAD contains plenty of garlic, which is thought to aid the respiratory system. Sweet red peppers provide a useful supply of immune-boosting vitamin C.

INGREDIENTS

Serves four

2 aubergines (eggplant)
2 red (bell) peppers
3–5 garlic cloves, chopped,
   or more to taste
2.5ml/½ tsp ground cumin
juice of ½–1 lemon, to taste
45–60ml/3–4 tbsp extra virgin olive oil
1–2 pinches of cayenne pepper
coarse sea salt
chopped fresh coriander (cilantro),
   to garnish
thinly sliced ciabatta bread,
   to serve (optional)

free from

✓	nuts
✓	dairy
	wheat
✓	seafood
✓	eggs
	yeast
	citrus
✓	alcohol

VARIATION

Other grilled (broiled) or barbecued vegetables would be good served with this salad – try wedges of red onion.

1 Place the aubergines and peppers directly over a medium-low gas flame, under a grill (broiler) or on a barbecue. Turn the vegetables frequently until they are deflated and the skins are evenly charred.

2 Put the aubergines and peppers in a plastic bag or in a bowl and seal tightly. Leave to cool for 30–40 minutes.

3 Peel the vegetables, roughly chop the flesh and reserve the juices. Put the flesh in a bowl with the juices, and add the garlic, cumin, lemon juice, olive oil, cayenne pepper and salt. Mix well. Tip the mixture into a serving bowl and garnish with coriander. Serve with bread, unless avoiding wheat or yeast.

NUTRITION NOTES

Per portion:

Energy	128Kcal/530kJ
Fat	9.3g
saturated fat	1.2g
Carbohydrate	9.1g
Fibre	4.4g
Calcium	29.6mg

spicy pumpkin dip

PUMPKIN IS AN EXCELLENT CHOICE for those suffering from asthma and eczema because it rarely causes allergies. It is also rich in betacarotene, which is thought to help the immune system.

INGREDIENTS

Serves six

45–60ml/3–4 tbsp olive oil
1 onion, finely chopped
3–4 garlic cloves, roughly chopped
675g/1½lb pumpkin, peeled
  and diced
5–10ml/1–2 tsp ground cumin
5ml/1 tsp paprika
1.5–2.5ml/¼–½ tsp ground ginger
1.5–2.5ml/¼–½ tsp curry powder
75g/3oz chopped canned tomatoes or
  diced fresh tomatoes and 15–30ml/
  1–2 tbsp tomato purée (paste)
½–1 red jalapeño or serrano chilli,
  chopped, or cayenne pepper,
  to taste
pinch of sugar
salt
chopped coriander (cilantro), to garnish

1 Heat the olive oil in a frying pan, add the onion and half the garlic and fry for about 5 minutes, stirring occasionally, until the onion is softened. Add the diced pumpkin to the pan, then cover and cook for about 10 minutes, stirring once or twice, or until the pumpkin is half-tender.

2 Add the spices to the pan and cook for 1–2 minutes. Stir in the tomatoes, chilli, sugar and salt and cook over a medium-high heat until the liquid has evaporated.

3 When the pumpkin is tender, mash to a coarse purée. Add the remaining garlic and taste for seasoning. Serve at room temperature, sprinkled with the coriander.

NUTRITION NOTES

Per portion:

Energy	82Kcal/338kJ
Fat	6g
saturated fat	0.8g
Carbohydrate	5.5g
Fibre	1.4g
Calcium	42mg

VARIATION

Use butternut squash, or any other winter squash, in place of the pumpkin.

free from

✓ nuts
✓ dairy
✓ wheat
✓ seafood
✓ eggs
✓ yeast
✓ citrus
✓ alcohol

guacamole

A RICH AND CREAMY DIP that provides vitamin C, which is essential for good health. Garlic and chillies are thought to help relieve congestion so may be beneficial for hayfever sufferers.

INGREDIENTS

Serves six

2 large, ripe avocados
2 red chillies, seeded
1 garlic clove
1 shallot
30ml/2 tbsp extra virgin olive oil, plus
   extra to serve
juice of 1 lemon
salt and ground black pepper
flat leaf parsley leaves, to garnish
vegetable crudités, such as cucumber,
   carrot, red pepper and celery,
   to serve

1 Cut the avocados in half and carefully remove the stones.

2 Scoop out the avocado flesh into a large mixing bowl, then using a fork or potato masher, mash the avocado flesh until smooth.

3 Finely chop the seeded chillies, garlic and shallot, then stir them into the mashed avocado with the olive oil and lemon juice. Season to taste.

4 Spoon the mixture into a small serving bowl. Drizzle over a little extra olive oil and scatter with a few flat leaf parsley leaves. Serve the dip immediately.

COOK'S TIP

This dish can be prepared with any other green vegetable that is in season, such as Swiss chard, fennel or Chinese leaves (Chinese cabbage).

NUTRITION NOTES

Per portion:

Energy	146Kcal/604kJ
Fat	15.1g
saturated fat	1.9g
Carbohydrate	1.6g
Fibre	2.1g
Calcium	9.9mg

free from
✓ nuts
✓ dairy
✓ wheat
✓ seafood
✓ eggs
✓ yeast
  citrus
✓ alcohol

spiced marinated herrings

THESE DELICIOUS MARINATED OILY FISH provide a valuable source of essential fatty acids, which can help improve skin quality for those suffering from eczema.

INGREDIENTS

Serves four

2–3 herrings, filleted
1 onion, sliced
juice of 1½–2 lemons
25ml/1½ tbsp sugar
10–15 black peppercorns
10–15 allspice berries
1.5ml/¼ tsp mustard seeds
3 bay leaves, torn
salt

1 Place the herrings in a shallow dish, cover with cold water and soak for about 5 minutes, then drain. Place in a shallow dish and pour over enough cold water to cover. Leave to soak for 2–3 hours, then drain. Pour over enough fresh cold water to cover and leave to soak overnight.

2 Hold the soaked herrings under cold running water and rinse them very thoroughly, both inside and out.

3 Cut each herring into bitesize pieces, then place the pieces in a glass bowl or shallow dish.

4 Sprinkle the onion over the fish, then add the lemon juice, sugar, peppercorns, allspice, mustard seeds, bay leaves and salt. Add enough water to just cover. Cover the bowl and chill for 2 days to allow the flavours to blend before serving.

NUTRITION NOTES

Per portion:	
Energy	233Kcal/971kJ
Fat	13.5g
saturated fat	2.2g
Carbohydrate	9.9g
Fibre	0.4g
Calcium	76.9mg

free from
✓ nuts
✓ dairy
✓ wheat
seafood
✓ eggs
✓ yeast
citrus
✓ alcohol

skewered lamb with red onion salsa

THESE LITTLE KEBABS are a perfect choice of appetizer for people avoiding potential allergens because lamb is one of the least allergenic foods known.

2 Cover the bowl with clear film and set aside in a cool place for a few hours, stirring once or twice.

3 Spear the lamb cubes on four small skewers – if using wooden skewers, soak them first in cold water for 30 minutes to prevent them from burning.

4 To make the salsa, put the sliced onion, tomato, red wine vinegar and basil or mint leaves in a small bowl and stir together until thoroughly blended. Season to taste with salt, garnish with mint, then set aside while you cook the lamb skewers.

5 Cook on a barbecue or under a preheated grill (broiler) for 5–10 minutes, turning frequently, until the lamb is well browned but still slightly pink in the centre. Serve hot, with the salsa.

INGREDIENTS

Serves four

225g/8oz lean lamb, cubed
2.5ml/½ tsp ground cumin
5ml/1 tsp paprika
15ml/1 tbsp olive oil
salt and ground black pepper

For the salsa

1 red onion, very thinly sliced
1 large tomato, seeded and chopped
15ml/1 tbsp red wine vinegar
3–4 fresh basil or mint leaves,
    coarsely torn
small mint leaves, to garnish

free from
✓ nuts
✓ dairy
✓ wheat
✓ seafood
✓ eggs
  yeast
✓ citrus
  alcohol

1 Place the lamb cubes, cumin, paprika and olive oil in a bowl. Season with salt and pepper and stir well.

NUTRITION NOTES

Per portion:

Energy	136Kcal/564kJ
Fat	7.8g
saturated fat	2.6g
Carbohydrate	4.1g
Fibre	0.7g
Calcium	29.1mg

shallot skewers with mustard dip

SHALLOTS ARE THOUGHT TO HAVE anti-inflammatory properties that can help combat the symptoms of asthma. These tasty skewers make an ideal start to a meal.

INGREDIENTS

Serves six

1kg/2¼lb small new potatoes, or larger
  potatoes halved
200g/7oz shallots, halved
30ml/2 tbsp olive oil
15ml/1 tbsp sea salt

For the dip

4 garlic cloves, crushed
2 egg yolks
30ml/2 tbsp lemon juice
300ml/½ pint/1¼ cups extra virgin
  olive oil
10ml/2 tsp wholegrain mustard
salt and ground black pepper

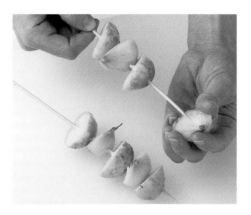

3 Par-cook the potatoes in their skins in boiling water for 5 minutes. Drain well and then thread them on to short skewers alternating them with the shallots.

4 Brush the skewers with oil and sprinkle with salt. Barbecue or grill for about 10 minutes, turning occasionally. Serve with the mustard dip.

NUTRITION NOTES

Per portion:	
Energy	592Kcal/2453kJ
Fat	51.7g
saturated fat	7.4g
Carbohydrate	28.7g
Fibre	2.4g
Calcium	29.6mg

1 Prepare a barbecue or preheat the grill (broiler). Place the garlic, egg yolks and lemon juice in a food processor or blender and process for a few seconds until smooth.

2 Keep the motor running and add the oil gradually, pouring it in a thin stream, until the mixture forms a thick, glossy cream. Stir in the mustard and season. Chill until ready to use.

COOK'S TIP

If eggs trigger your condition, then try serving these skewers with a fresh tomato salsa.

free from

✓ nuts
✓ dairy
✓ wheat
✓ seafood
  eggs
  yeast
  citrus
  alcohol

spinach and rice soup

THIS NUTRITIOUS SOUP makes a substantial appetizer or a healthy lunch or supper for sufferers of asthma, eczema and hayfever. For those with an intolerance or allergy to dairy products, simply omit the shavings of cheese.

2 Either chop the spinach finely using a large kitchen knife or place in a food processor and process the leaves to a fairly coarse purée.

3 Heat the oil in a large pan and gently cook the onion, garlic and chilli for 4–5 minutes until softened. Stir in the rice until well coated, then pour in the stock and reserved spinach liquid. Bring to the boil, lower the heat and simmer for 10 minutes.

INGREDIENTS

Serves four

675g/1½lb fresh spinach leaves, washed
30ml/2 tbsp extra virgin olive oil
1 small onion, finely chopped
2 garlic cloves, finely chopped
1 small fresh red chilli, seeded and
  finely chopped
225g/8oz/generous 1 cup risotto rice
1.2 litres/2 pints/5 cups fresh stock
salt and freshly ground black pepper
shavings of pared Parmesan or Pecorino
  cheese, to serve (optional)

1 Place the spinach in a large pan with just the water that clings to its leaves after washing. Add a large pinch of salt. Heat gently until the spinach has wilted, turning it occasionally with a wooden spoon, then remove the pan from the heat and drain, reserving any liquid from the pan.

free from
- ✓ nuts
- dairy
- ✓ wheat
- ✓ seafood
- ✓ eggs
- yeast
- ✓ citrus
- ✓ alcohol

COOK'S TIP
Risotto rice gives this soup a lovely creamy texture, but you could use long grain rice instead.

NUTRITION NOTES

Per portion:

Energy	296Kcal/1232kJ
Fat	7.5g
saturated fat	1.1g
Carbohydrate	49g
Fibre	4.8g
Calcium	335.9mg

4 Add the spinach, with salt and pepper to taste. Cook for 5–7 minutes, until the rice is tender. Check the seasoning. Serve in heated bowls, topped with the shavings of cheese, if you like.

roasted garlic and squash soup

BUTTERNUT SQUASH is rich in immune-boosting betacarotene, while tomatoes provide a good supply of vitamin C, which can help to fight histamines. Garlic is a natural decongestant and may help to alleviate the symptoms of hayfever.

INGREDIENTS

Serves four

2 garlic bulbs, outer papery skin removed
75ml/5 tbsp olive oil
a few fresh thyme sprigs
1 butternut squash, halved and seeded
2 onions, chopped
5ml/1 tsp ground coriander
1.2 litres/2 pints/5 cups fresh chicken stock
45ml/3 tbsp chopped fresh oregano
salt and ground black pepper

For the salsa

4 large ripe tomatoes, halved and seeded
1 red pepper, halved and seeded
1 large fresh red chilli, halved and seeded
30–45ml/2–3 tbsp extra virgin olive oil

1 Preheat the oven to 220°C/425°F/ Gas 7. Place the garlic bulbs on a piece of foil and pour over half the oil. Add the thyme, then fold over the foil to enclose the garlic. Place on a baking sheet with the squash, then brush the squash with 15ml/ 1 tbsp of the remaining olive oil. Add the tomatoes, pepper and chilli for the salsa.

2 Roast for 25 minutes, then remove the tomatoes, pepper and chilli. Reduce the oven temperature to 190°C/375°F/Gas 5 and cook the squash and garlic for 20–25 minutes more, or until the squash is tender.

3 Heat the remaining oil in a pan add the onions and coriander and cook for 10 minutes, or until the onion has softened.

4 Skin the pepper and chilli and process in a food processor or blender with the tomatoes and the olive oil. Season to taste.

5 Squeeze the roasted garlic out of its papery skin into the onions and scoop the squash out of its skin, adding it to the pan. Add the stock, 5ml/1 tsp salt and plenty of black pepper. Bring to the boil and simmer for 10 minutes. Then stir in half the fresh oregano. Leave the soup to cool slightly, then process in a food processor or blender (in batches if necessary) or press the soup through a fine sieve.

6 Reheat the soup over a medium heat without allowing it to boil, then taste for seasoning before ladling it into warmed bowls. Top each portion with a spoonful of salsa and sprinkle over the remaining chopped fresh oregano.

NUTRITION NOTES

Per portion:	
Energy	202Kcal/835kJ
Fat	14.3g
saturated fat	2g
Carbohydrate	15.4g
Fibre	2.6g
Calcium	142.9mg

free from

✓ nuts
✓ dairy
✓ wheat
✓ seafood
✓ eggs
✓ yeast
✓ citrus
✓ alcohol

spicy black-eyed bean soup

A FILLING AND SATISFYING SOUP which is a good source of low-fat protein and fibre. Beans provide complex B vitamins, which can improve skin quality, and onions, with their natural anti-inflammatory properties, are believed to help those with asthma.

INGREDIENTS

Serves four

175g/6oz/1 cup black-eyed beans (peas)
15ml/1 tbsp olive oil
2 onions, chopped
4 garlic cloves, chopped
1 medium-hot or 2–3 mild fresh
    chillies, chopped
5ml/1 tsp ground cumin
5ml/1 tsp ground turmeric
250g/9oz fresh or canned
    tomatoes, diced
600ml/1 pint/2½ cups fresh chicken, beef
    or vegetable stock
25g/1oz fresh coriander (cilantro) leaves,
    roughly chopped
pitta bread, to serve (optional)

1 Put the black-eyed beans in a pan, cover with cold water, bring to the boil, then cook for 5 minutes. Remove from the heat, cover and leave to stand for 2 hours. Drain the beans, return them to the pan, cover with fresh cold water, then simmer for 35–40 minutes, or until the beans are tender. Drain and set aside.

free from
✓ nuts
✓ dairy
  wheat
✓ seafood
✓ eggs
  yeast
✓ citrus
✓ alcohol

VARIATION

If you like, substitute other beans such as haricot or cannellini beans for the black-eyed beans.

2 Heat the oil in a pan, add the onions, garlic and chilli and cook for about 5 minutes, or until the onion is soft. Stir in the cumin, turmeric, tomatoes, stock, half the coriander and the beans and simmer for 20–30 minutes. Stir in the remaining coriander and serve at once with pitta bread, if you are not allergic to wheat or yeast.

COOK'S TIP

If you are in a hurry and don't have time to soak and cook the black-eyed beans, then use a 400g/14oz can instead. Simply drain and rinse the beans thoroughly in cold water, then add to the soup in step 2.

NUTRITION NOTES

Per portion:	
Energy	202Kcal/854kJ
Fat	4.2g
saturated fat	0.5g
Carbohydrate	31g
Fibre	9.1g
Calcium	140.5mg

a potage of lentils and garlic

THIS NOURISHING SOUP makes a perfect addition to a healthy diet and is an ideal lunch or supper dish. Maintaining a healthy diet helps to protect against colds and viruses that can trigger asthma.

INGREDIENTS

Serves four

30ml/2 tbsp olive oil
1 onion, chopped
2 celery sticks, chopped
1–2 carrots, sliced
8 garlic cloves, chopped
1 potato, peeled and diced
250g/9oz/generous 1 cup red lentils
1 litre/1¾ pints/4 cups fresh vegetable
    or chicken stock
2 bay leaves
1–2 lemons, halved
2.5ml/½ tsp ground cumin, or
    to taste
cayenne pepper, to taste
salt and ground black pepper
lemon slices and chopped fresh flat leaf
    parsley leaves, to serve

1 Heat the oil in a large pan. Add the onion and cook for about 5 minutes, or until softened, stirring occasionally. Stir in the celery, carrots, half the garlic and all the potato. Cook for a few minutes, stirring once or twice, until the vegetables begin to soften.

2 Add the lentils and stock to the pan and bring to the boil. Reduce the heat, cover and simmer for about 30 minutes, or until the potato and lentils are tender.

3 Add the bay leaves, remaining chopped garlic and half the lemons to the pan and cook the soup for a further 10 minutes. Remove the bay leaves from the pan. Squeeze the juice from the remaining lemons, then stir into the soup, to taste.

4 Pour the soup into a food processor or blender and process until smooth. (You may need to do this in batches.) Tip the soup back into the pan, stir in the cumin, cayenne pepper, and season with salt and pepper.

5 Ladle the soup into bowls and top each portion with lemon slices and a sprinkling of flat leaf parsley.

NUTRITION NOTES

Per portion:	
Energy	321Kcal/1357kJ
Fat	7g
saturated fat	0.8g
Carbohydrate	49g
Fibre	5.3g
Calcium	122.3mg

free from

✓ nuts
✓ dairy
✓ wheat
✓ seafood
✓ eggs
✓ yeast
  citrus
✓ alcohol

chicken and leek soup with prunes

THIS TASTY, WHOLESOME SOUP is packed with fresh vegetables essential for a healthy immune system. Try and use organic produce if possible.

3 Add the chicken fillets and cook for a further 30 minutes until they are just cooked. Leave until cool enough to handle, then strain the stock. Reserve the chicken fillets and the meat from the chicken carcass. Discard all the skin, bones, cooked vegetables and herbs. Skim as much fat as you can from the stock, then return the stock to the pan.

4 Meanwhile, rinse the pearl barley thoroughly in a sieve under cold running water, then cook it in a large pan of boiling water for about 10 minutes. Drain the barley in a sieve, rinse well again and drain thoroughly.

5 Add the pearl barley to the stock. Bring to the boil over a medium heat, then lower the heat and cook very gently for 15–20 minutes, or until the barley is just cooked and tender. Season the soup with 5ml/1 tsp salt and black pepper.

6 Add the prunes. Slice the remaining leeks and add them to the pan. Bring to the boil, then simmer for 10 minutes, or until the leeks are just cooked.

7 Slice the chicken fillets and add them to the soup with the remaining chicken meat, sliced or cut into neat pieces. Reheat if necessary, then ladle the soup into deep plates and sprinkle with chopped parsley.

INGREDIENTS

Serves Six

1 chicken, weighing about 2kg/4¼lb
900g/2lb leeks
1 bay leaf and a few each fresh parsley stalks and thyme sprigs
1 large carrot, thickly sliced
2.4 litres/4 pints/10 cups fresh chicken or beef stock
115g/4oz/generous ½ cup pearl barley
400g/14oz ready-to-eat prunes
salt and ground black pepper
chopped fresh parsley, to garnish

free from
✓ nuts
✓ dairy
✓ wheat
✓ seafood
✓ eggs
  yeast
✓ citrus
✓ alcohol

1 Cut the breast fillets off the chicken and set aside. Place the remaining chicken carcass in a large pan. Cut half the leeks into 5cm/2in lengths and add them to the pan.

2 Tie the bay leaf, parsley and thyme into a bouquet garni and add to the pan with the carrot and the stock. Bring to the boil, then reduce the heat and cover. Simmer gently for 1 hour. Skim off any scum when the water first boils and occasionally during simmering.

NUTRITION NOTES

Per portion:

Energy	341Kcal/1445kJ
Fat	3.9g
saturated fat	0.9g
Carbohydrate	45.4g
Fibre	7.6g
Calcium	131.7mg

chinese chicken and chilli soup

THE AROMATIC SPICES in this light and tasty soup may help to ease nasal congestion. Skinless chicken breast offers a good source of healthy low-fat protein.

INGREDIENTS

Serves six

150g/5oz boneless, skinless chicken breast portion, cut crossways into thin strips

2.5cm/1in piece fresh root ginger, finely chopped

5cm/2in piece lemon grass stalk, finely chopped

1 red chilli, seeded and thinly sliced

8 baby corn cobs, halved lengthwise

1 large carrot, scrubbed or peeled and cut into thin sticks

1 litre/1¾ pints/4 cups hot, fresh chicken stock

4 spring onions (scallions), thinly sliced

12 small shiitake mushrooms, sliced

115g/4oz/1 cup vermicelli rice noodles

30ml/2 tbsp tamari

salt

ground black pepper

2 Place the pot in an unheated oven. Set the temperature to 200°C/400°F/ Gas 6 and cook the soup for 30–40 minutes. Add the spring onions and mushrooms, cover and return to the oven for 10 minutes.

3 Soak the noodles following the packet instructions. Drain and divide among four bowls. Stir the tamari into the soup, then season and pour into the bowls. Serve immediately.

NUTRITION NOTES

Per portion:	
Energy	112Kcal/470kJ
Fat	0.6g
saturated fat	0.1g
Carbohydrate	19.1g
Fibre	0.9g
Calcium	43.2mg

1 Place the chicken strips, fresh root ginger, lemon grass and red chilli in a Chinese sand pot. Add the halved baby corn and the carrot sticks. Pour over the hot chicken stock and cover the pot.

free from

✓ nuts

✓ dairy

✓ wheat

✓ seafood

✓ eggs

  yeast

✓ citrus

✓ alcohol

meat, poultry
and fish

The dishes in this chapter are inspiring — they each have their specific health-promoting properties. For a low-allergy meat, choose chicken or lamb. Try chicken, carrot and leek parcels to boost your immunity or roasted chicken with grapes and fresh root ginger to prevent respiratory infections. Braised shoulder of lamb with pearl barley is rich in valuable nutrients and lamb boulangère is ideal for asthma sufferers. Fish dishes include peppered salmon fillets baked with potatoes and thyme, a valuable source of essential fatty acids that help maintain healthy skin and baked sea bass with lemon grass and red onions, which contains spices that may help ease nasal congestion.

chicken, carrot and leek parcels

BAKING LOW-ALLERGEN chicken and vegetables in paper parcels is incredibly healthy. It helps to retain the valuable nutrients that are needed for good health.

INGREDIENTS

Serves four

4 chicken fillets or skinless, boneless
    breast portions
2 small leeks, sliced
2 carrots, grated
2 stoned black olives, chopped
1 garlic clove, crushed
salt and black pepper
black olives and fresh herb sprigs,
    to garnish

1 Preheat the oven to 200°C/400°F/ Gas 6. Season the chicken well. Cut out four sheets of lightly greased greaseproof (wax) paper about 23cm/9in square. Divide the leeks equally among them. Put a piece of chicken on top of each portion of leeks.

COOK'S TIP
Small, skinless turkey breast fillets also work well in this recipe.

2 Mix the grated carrots, chopped olives and crushed garlic together. Season lightly and place on top of the chicken portions, dividing them equally.

3 Carefully wrap up each parcel, making sure that the paper folds are sealed. Place the parcels on a baking sheet and bake for 20 minutes. Serve hot, in the paper, garnished with black olives and fresh herb sprigs.

free from
✓ nuts
✓ dairy
✓ wheat
✓ seafood
✓ eggs
✓ yeast
✓ citrus
✓ alcohol

NUTRITION NOTES

Per portion:

Energy	190Kcal/804kJ
Fat	2.8g
saturated fat	0.6g
Carbohydrate	6.6g
Fibre	2.9g
Calcium	42.2mg

chicken breasts with chilli salsa

| THESE DELICIOUS marinated chicken breasts make a good allergy-free choice. The tomato salsa offers a good source of health-promoting vitamin C.

INGREDIENTS

Serves four

4 chicken breast portions, about 175g/
  6oz each, boned and skinned
30ml/2 tbsp fresh lemon juice
30ml/2 tbsp olive oil
10ml/2 tsp ground cumin
10ml/2 tsp dried oregano
15ml/1 tbsp coarse
  black pepper
salt

For the salsa

1 fresh hot green chilli
450g/1lb tomatoes, seeded
  and chopped
3 spring onions (scallions), chopped
15ml/1 tbsp chopped fresh parsley
30ml/2 tbsp chopped fresh
  coriander (cilantro)
30ml/2 tbsp fresh lemon juice
45ml/3 tbsp olive oil
5ml/1 tsp salt

1 With a meat mallet, pound the chicken between sheets of clear film until thin.

2 In a shallow dish, combine the lemon juice, oil, cumin, oregano and pepper. Add the chicken and turn to coat. Cover and leave to stand in a cool place for at least 2 hours, or place in the refrigerator and chill overnight.

3 To make the salsa, char the chilli skin either over a gas flame or under the grill (broiler). Leave to cool for 5 minutes. Wearing rubber gloves, carefully rub off the charred skin from the chillies. For a less hot flavour, discard the seeds.

4 Chop the chilli very finely and place in a bowl. Add the tomatoes, spring onions, parsley, coriander, lemon juice, olive oil and salt and mix well.

5 Remove the chicken from the marinade and then season lightly.

6 Heat a ridged grill pan. Add the chicken breasts and cook for about 3 minutes until browned on one side. Turn them over and cook for 3–4 minutes more. Serve with the chilli salsa.

NUTRITION NOTES

Per portion:	
Energy	323Kcal/1352kJ
Fat	16.5g
saturated fat	2.5g
Carbohydrate	8.3g
Fibre	1.2g
Calcium	107.7mg

free from
✓ nuts
✓ dairy
✓ wheat
✓ seafood
✓ eggs
✓ yeast
  citrus
✓ alcohol

spinach and potato stuffed chicken

THE SPINACH STUFFING and tomato sauce both offer a good supply of vitamin C, which is recommended for its ability to boost immunity and combat histamine.

INGREDIENTS

Serves six

115g/4oz floury potatoes, diced
115g/4oz spinach leaves, finely chopped
1 egg, beaten
30ml/2 tbsp chopped fresh
 coriander (cilantro)
4 large chicken breasts
30ml/2 tbsp olive oil
mushrooms, to serve (optional)

For the sauce

400g/14oz can chopped tomatoes
1 garlic clove, crushed
150ml/¼ pint/⅔ cup fresh chicken stock
30ml/2 tbsp chopped fresh coriander
 (cilantro)
salt and ground black pepper

1 Preheat the oven to 180°C/350°F/ Gas 4. Boil the potatoes in a pan of boiling water for 15 minutes, or until tender. Drain them and roughly mash with a fork. Stir the spinach into the potato with the egg and coriander, then season to taste.

2 Cut almost all the way through the chicken breasts and open them out to form a pocket in each. Spoon the filling into the centre and fold the chicken back over again. Secure with cocktail sticks (toothpicks) and place in a roasting pan.

3 Sprinkle the chicken with the olive oil and cover. Bake for 25 minutes, then remove the foil and cook for 10 minutes, or until the chicken is brown and cooked.

4 While the chicken is cooking, make the sauce. Boil the tomatoes, garlic and stock rapidly for 10 minutes. Season and stir in the coriander. Serve with the chicken and mushrooms, if you like.

COOK'S TIP
Young spinach leaves have a sweet flavour and are ideal for this dish.

NUTRITION NOTES

Per portion:

Energy	202Kcal/848kJ
Fat	6.2g
saturated fat	1.2g
Carbohydrate	5.7g
Fibre	1.4g
Calcium	60.9mg

free from

✓ nuts
✓ dairy
✓ wheat
✓ seafood
 eggs
 yeast
✓ citrus
✓ alcohol

slow-cooked chicken and potatoes

THIS FLAVOURFUL CHICKEN DISH contains plenty of onions, which are recommended for asthma. Sufferers are encouraged to try to eat an onion a day.

INGREDIENTS

Serves four

25g/1oz/2 tbsp butter, plus extra
   for greasing
15ml/1 tbsp vegetable oil
2 large bacon slices, chopped
4 large chicken joints, halved
1kg/2¼lb baking potatoes, cut into
   5mm/¼in slices
2 large onions, thinly sliced
15ml/1 tbsp chopped fresh thyme
600ml/1 pint/2½ cups fresh chicken stock
1 bay leaf
salt and ground black pepper

1 Heat the butter and oil in a large heavy frying pan, add the bacon and chicken and brown on all sides, stirring frequently.

2 Arrange half the potato slices in a large, lightly greased, flameproof baking dish.

3 Preheat the oven to 150°C/300°F/ Gas 2. Cover the potatoes with half the onions. Sprinkle with half the thyme, and season well. Using a slotted spoon, transfer the chicken and bacon to the baking dish. Reserve the fat in the pan.

4 Sprinkle the remaining thyme over the chicken, season, then cover with the remaining onion slices, followed by a layer of potato slices. Season again. Pour in the stock, add the bay leaf and brush the potatoes with the reserved fat from the pan.

COOK'S TIP
Instead of chicken joints, use eight chicken thighs or chicken drumsticks.

5 Cover tightly and bake for 2 hours, or until the chicken is tender. Preheat the grill (broiler). Take the cover off the baking dish and place it under the grill until the potato is just turning golden brown and crisp. Remove the bay leaf and serve hot.

NUTRITION NOTES

Per portion:

Energy	714Kcal/2990kJ
Fat	36.8g
saturated fat	12.2g
Carbohydrate	50.8g
Fibre	4.5g
Calcium	82.4mg

free from
✓ nuts
dairy
✓ wheat
✓ seafood
✓ eggs
✓ yeast
✓ citrus
✓ alcohol

roasted chicken with grapes and fresh root ginger

THE TASTY GRAPE STUFFING in this dish is a good choice for people avoiding wheat and nuts, which are often found in classic meat stuffings.

INGREDIENTS

Serves four

1–1.6kg/2¼–3½lb chicken
115–130g/4–4½oz fresh root ginger, grated
6–8 garlic cloves, roughly chopped
about 30ml/2 tbsp olive oil
2–3 large pinches of ground cinnamon
500g/1¼lb seeded red and green grapes
500g/1¼lb seedless green grapes
5–7 shallots, chopped
250ml/8fl oz/1 cup fresh chicken stock
salt and ground black pepper

1 Rub the chicken with half of the grated ginger, the chopped garlic, olive oil, cinnamon, salt and lots of black pepper. Leave to marinate in a cool place for about 1 hour.

2 Halve and seed the red and green seeded grapes and mix them with the seedless grapes.

COOK'S TIP

Always wash grapes thoroughly to remove dust, yeast and pesticides that are often present on grape skin.

3 Preheat the oven to 180°C/350°F/ Gas 4. Heat a heavy frying pan or flameproof casserole until hot.

4 Remove the chicken from the marinade, add to the pan or casserole and cook until browned on all sides. (There should be enough oil on the chicken to brown it but, if not, add a little extra.)

5 Put some of the shallots into the chicken cavity with the garlic and ginger from the marinade and as many of the red and green grapes that will fit inside. Roast in the oven in a roasting pan or casserole for 40–60 minutes, or until the chicken is tender and thoroughly cooked.

6 Remove the chicken from the pan and keep warm. Pour off any oil from the pan, and tip any sediment into a frying pan. Add the remaining shallots to the pan and cook, stirring occasionally, for 5 minutes.

7 Add half the remaining grapes, the remaining ginger, the stock and any chicken juices. Cook over a medium-high heat until the grapes have cooked down to a thick sauce. Season to taste.

8 Serve the chicken on a large, warmed serving dish, with the sauce and reserved grapes.

free from

✓ nuts
✓ dairy
✓ wheat
✓ seafood
✓ eggs
  yeast
✓ citrus
✓ alcohol

NUTRITION NOTES

Per portion:

Energy	492Kcal/2051kJ
Fat	20.6g
saturated fat	5.7g
Carbohydrate	44.6g
Fibre	0.5g
Calcium	70.5mg

braised shoulder of lamb

| THIS WARMING, HEARTY WINTER STEW is rich in valuable nutrients and provides plenty of fibre.

INGREDIENTS

Serves four

45ml/3 tbsp olive oil
1 large onion, chopped
2 garlic cloves, chopped
2 celery sticks, sliced
a little plain (all-purpose) flour
675g/1½lb boned shoulder of lamb,
  cut into cubes
1 litre/1¾ pints/4 cups fresh lamb stock
115g/4oz/⅔ cup pearl barley
225g/8oz baby carrots
225g/8oz baby turnips
salt and ground black pepper
30ml/2 tbsp chopped fresh marjoram,
  to garnish

1 Heat 30ml/2 tbsp of the oil in a flameproof casserole. Cook the onion and garlic until softened, add the celery, then cook until the vegetables brown.

2 Season the flour and toss the lamb in it. Use a slotted spoon to remove the vegetables from the casserole.

3 Add and heat the remaining oil with the juices in the casserole. Brown the lamb in batches until golden. When all the meat is browned, return it to the casserole with the onion mixture.

4 Add 900ml/1½ pints/3¾ cups of the stock to the casserole. Add the pearl barley. Cover, then bring to the boil, reduce the heat and simmer for 1 hour, or until the pearl barley and lamb are tender.

5 Add the baby carrots and turnips to the casserole for the final 15 minutes of cooking. Stir the meat occasionally during cooking and add the remaining stock, if necessary. Season to taste, and serve piping hot, garnished with marjoram.

free from
✓ nuts
✓ dairy
  wheat
✓ seafood
✓ eggs
✓ yeast
✓ citrus
✓ alcohol

NUTRITION NOTES

Per portion:

Energy	642Kcal/2678kJ
Fat	40.4g
saturated fat	16.9g
Carbohydrate	36.8g
Fibre	4g
Calcium	129.2mg

lamb boulangère

NON-ALLERGENIC LAMB AND POTATOES are teamed with fragrant herbs in this mouthwatering dish.

INGREDIENTS

Serves six

50g/2oz/¼ cup butter, plus extra
   for greasing
4–6 garlic cloves
2 yellow onions, thinly sliced
12–18 small fresh thyme or
   rosemary sprigs
2 fresh bay leaves
1.8kg/4lb red potatoes, thinly sliced
450ml/¾ pint/scant 2 cups hot, fresh
   lamb or vegetable stock
2kg/4½lb leg of lamb
30ml/2 tbsp olive oil
salt and ground black pepper

1 Preheat the oven to 190°C/375°F/ Gas 5. Use a little butter to grease a large baking dish, about 6cm/2½in deep. Finely chop half the garlic and sprinkle a little over the prepared dish.

2 Fry the onions in 25g/1oz/2 tbsp of the butter for 5–8 minutes, or until softened. Roughly chop half the thyme or rosemary and crush the bay leaves.

3 Arrange a layer of potatoes in the dish, then season well and sprinkle with half the remaining chopped garlic, half the thyme or rosemary and bay leaves, and all of the onions. Add the remaining potatoes in an even layer and then scatter over the rest of the chopped garlic and herbs.

NUTRITION NOTES

Per portion:	
Energy	867Kcal/3627kJ
Fat	39.6g
saturated fat	18.5g
Carbohydrate	55.7g
Fibre	4.6g
Calcium	81.4mg

4 Pour in the stock plus a little hot water, if necessary, to bring the liquid to just below the level of the potatoes. Dot with the remaining butter, cover with foil and cook for 40 minutes. Increase the temperature to 200°C/400°F/Gas 6.

5 Meanwhile, cut the rest of the garlic into slivers. Make small slits all over the lamb with a narrow, sharp knife and insert slivers of garlic and sprigs of thyme or rosemary into the slits. Season the lamb well with salt and plenty of pepper.

6 Uncover the potatoes and scatter a few rosemary or thyme sprigs over them. Rest a roasting rack or ovenproof cooling rack over the dish and place the lamb on it. Rub the olive oil over the meat.

7 Return the lamb to the oven and cook, turning it once or twice, for 1½–1¾ hours, depending on how well done you prefer lamb. Leave it to rest for 20 minutes in a warm place, before carving.

free from
✓ nuts
  dairy
✓ wheat
✓ seafood
✓ eggs
✓ yeast
✓ citrus
✓ alcohol

lamb shanks with beans and herbs

THIS LOW-ALLERGY DISH is perfect for those suffering from asthma and eczema. It contains anti-inflammatory onions, betacarotene and vitamin C for a healthy respiratory system, and B vitamins for healthy skin.

INGREDIENTS

Serves four

175g/6oz/1 cup dried cannellini beans, soaked overnight in cold water
150ml/¼ pint/⅔ cup water
45ml/3 tbsp olive oil
4 large lamb shanks, about 225g/8oz each
1 large onion, chopped
450g/1lb carrots, cut into thick chunks
2 celery sticks, cut into thick chunks
450g/1lb tomatoes, quartered
250ml/8fl oz/1 cup fresh vegetable stock
4 fresh rosemary sprigs
2 bay leaves
salt and ground black pepper

1 Soak a large clay pot in cold water for 20 minutes, drain. Drain and rinse the beans, place in a large pan of unsalted boiling water, boil rapidly for 10 minutes, then drain.

2 Place the water in the clay pot and add the drained beans.

3 Heat 30ml/2 tbsp of the olive oil in a large frying pan, add the lamb and cook over a high heat, turning occasionally until brown on all sides. Remove the lamb with a slotted spoon and set aside.

4 Add the remaining oil to the pan, then add the onion and cook gently for 5 minutes until softened.

COOK'S TIP
If you don't have an unglazed clay pot, then simply use any large, shallow baking dish. Unglazed dishes must be soaked but, if the dish is glazed, there is no need to soak it before baking.

5 Add the carrots and celery to the pan and cook for 2–3 minutes. Stir in the tomatoes and stock and mix well. Transfer the vegetables to the pot and season well. Add the rosemary and bay leaves and stir.

6 Place the lamb shanks on top of the beans and vegetables. Cover the clay pot and place it in an unheated oven. Set the oven to 220°C/425°F/Gas 7 and cook for about 30 minutes, or until the liquid is bubbling.

7 Reduce the oven temperature to 160°C/325°F/Gas 3 and cook for about 1½ hours, or until the meat is tender. Check the seasoning and serve on warmed plates, placing each lamb shank on a bed of beans and vegetables.

free from
- ✓ nuts
- ✓ dairy
- ✓ wheat
- ✓ seafood
- ✓ eggs
- ✓ yeast
- ✓ citrus
- ✓ alcohol

NUTRITION NOTES

Per portion:

Energy	606Kcal/2532kJ
Fat	31.3g
saturated fat	11.9g
Carbohydrate	38.2g
Fibre	12.1g
Calcium	159.7mg

peppered salmon fillets baked with potatoes and thyme

THIS SIMPLE FISH DISH offers a valuable supply of essential fatty acids, which can help maintain healthy skin.

INGREDIENTS

Serves four

675g/1½lb waxy potatoes, thinly sliced
1 onion, thinly sliced
10ml/2 tsp fresh thyme leaves
450ml/¾ pint/scant 2 cups fresh
   vegetable or fish stock
45ml/3 tbsp olive oil
4 skinless salmon fillets, about
   150g/5oz each
15ml/1 tbsp black peppercorns,
   roughly crushed
salt and ground black pepper
fresh thyme, to garnish
mangetouts (snow peas), to serve

1 Soak a fish clay pot in cold water for 20 minutes, then drain.

2 Layer the potato and onion slices in the clay pot, seasoning each layer and sprinkling with thyme. Pour over the vegetable or fish stock, sprinkle with half the oil, then cover and place in an unheated oven.

3 Set the oven to 190°C/375°F/Gas 5. Put the potatoes and onions in the unheated oven and cook for 40 minutes, then remove the lid and bake for a further 20 minutes, or until they are almost cooked through.

4 Meanwhile, brush the salmon fillets with the remaining olive oil and coat with the roughly crushed black peppercorns, pressing them in, if necessary, with the back of a spoon. Place the peppered salmon on top of the potatoes, cover and cook for 15 minutes, or until the salmon is opaque, removing the lid for the last 5 minutes. Garnish the salmon and potatoes with fresh thyme sprigs and serve with mangetouts.

free from

✓ nuts
✓ dairy
✓ wheat
   seafood
✓ eggs
✓ yeast
✓ citrus
✓ alcohol

NUTRITION NOTES

Per portion:

Energy	499Kcal/2087kJ
Fat	25.4g
saturated fat	5.5g
Carbohydrate	34.6g
Fibre	2.6g
Calcium	88mg

roast cod with pancetta and white beans

| LOW-ALLERGEN COD is preferable to fish with higher histamine levels such as mackerel.

INGREDIENTS

Serves four

200g/7oz/1 cup butter (lima) beans,
　soaked overnight in cold water to cover
2 leeks, thinly sliced
2 garlic cloves, chopped
8 fresh sage leaves
60ml/4 tbsp fruity olive oil
8 thin pancetta slices
4 thick cod steaks, skinned
12 cherry tomatoes
salt and ground black pepper

1 Drain the beans, tip into a pan and cover with cold water. Bring to the boil and skim off the foam on the surface.

2 Lower the heat, then stir in the leeks, garlic, 4 sage leaves and 30ml/2 tbsp of the olive oil. Simmer for 1–1½ hours until the beans are tender, adding more water if necessary. Drain, return to the pan, season, stir in 15ml/1 tbsp olive oil and keep warm.

3 Preheat the oven to 200°C/400°F/ Gas 6. Wrap two slices of pancetta around the edge of each cod steak, tying it on with fine kitchen string or securing it with a wooden cocktail stick (toothpick). Insert a sage leaf between the pancetta and the cod. Season the fish with salt and pepper.

4 Heat a frying pan, add 15ml/1 tbsp of the remaining olive oil and sear the cod steaks for 1 minute on each side. Transfer to an ovenproof dish and roast for 5 minutes.

5 Add the tomatoes and drizzle over the remaining olive oil. Roast for 5 minutes more until the cod steaks are cooked but still juicy. Serve with the butter beans and roasted tomatoes. Garnish with parsley.

NUTRITION NOTES

Per portion:

Energy	497Kcal/2086kJ
Fat	22.4g
saturated fat	5.5g
Carbohydrate	29.7g
Fibre	9.7g
Calcium	80.4mg

free from
✓ nuts
✓ dairy
✓ wheat
　seafood
✓ eggs
✓ yeast
✓ citrus
✓ alcohol

baked sea bass with lemon grass and red onions

THE SPICES IN THIS TASTY DISH may help to ease nasal congestion. Sea bass is a good source of low-fat protein.

INGREDIENTS

Serves two

1 sea bass, about 675g/1½lb, cleaned
  and scaled
30ml/2 tbsp olive oil
2 lemon grass stalks,
  finely sliced
1 red onion, finely shredded
1 chilli, seeded and finely chopped
5cm/2in piece fresh root ginger,
  finely shredded
45ml/3 tbsp chopped fresh
  coriander (cilantro)
rind and juice of 2 limes
30ml/2 tbsp tamari
salt and ground black pepper
steamed rice and sugar snap peas,
  to serve

1 Soak a fish clay pot in cold water for 20 minutes, then drain. Make four to five diagonal slashes on both sides of the fish. Repeat the slashes on one side in the opposite direction to give an attractive cross-hatched effect. Rub the sea bass inside and out with salt, pepper and 15ml/1 tbsp of the olive oil.

2 Mix together the lemon grass, onion, chilli, ginger, coriander and lime rind.

3 Place a little of the lemon grass and red onion mixture in the base of the clay pot, then lay the fish on top. Sprinkle the remaining mixture over the fish, then sprinkle over the lime juice, tamari and the remaining olive oil. Cover and place in an unheated oven.

4 Set the oven to 220°C/425°F/Gas 7 and place the spiced sea bass in the unheated oven. Cook for 30–40 minutes, or until the flesh flakes easily when tested with a sharp knife. Serve immediately with steamed rice and sugar snap peas.

NUTRITION NOTES

Per portion:

Energy	395Kcal/1652kJ
Fat	17.7g
saturated fat	2.7g
Carbohydrate	8.1g
Fibre	0.9g
Calcium	379.8mg

free from
✓ nuts
✓ dairy
✓ wheat
  seafood
✓ eggs
✓ yeast
  citrus
✓ alcohol

baked sardines with caper and tomato stuffing

FOR THOSE AVOIDING WHEAT, serve the stuffed sardines with rice or potatoes instead of crusty bread.

INGREDIENTS

Serves four

16 fresh sardines, cleaned
8–12 cherry tomatoes,
   on the vine, sliced
45ml/3 tbsp capers, chopped
½ small red onion, very finely chopped
60ml/4 tbsp olive oil
grated rind and juice 1 lemon
45ml/3 tbsp chopped fresh parsley
15ml/1 tbsp chopped fresh basil
basil sprigs and lemon wedges,
   to garnish
crusty bread, to serve

1 Remove the backbone from each sardine by placing it slit side down on a chopping board. Using your fingers, push firmly along the length of the backbone to loosen it from the flesh. Turn the sardine over and pull out the bone; cut the ends with a sharp knife to release it. Repeat with the remaining sardines.

2 Place the tomato slices inside each sardine; they may stick out slightly, depending on the size of the fish. Mix the capers and red onion together and place on top of the tomatoes.

3 Preheat the oven to 200°C/400°F/ Gas 6. Lay the sardines in a single layer in a large shallow baking dish.

4 Mix together the oil, lemon rind and juice and herbs.

COOK'S TIP
Removing the bones before cooking, as in step 1 of this recipe, makes the sardines easier to eat.

5 Drizzle the mixture over the sardines. Bake for 10 minutes until just cooked.

6 Garnish with basil and lemon wedges and serve with crusty bread.

NUTRITION NOTES

Per portion:

Energy	347Kcal/1444kJ
Fat	24.2g
saturated fat	4.1g
Carbohydrate	2.6g
Fibre	1g
Calcium	171.4mg

free from

✓	nuts
✓	dairy
	wheat
	seafood
✓	eggs
	yeast
	citrus
✓	alcohol

scallops with garlic and chilli

SCALLOPS ARE A GOOD SOURCE of the valuable mineral zinc, which is recommended for people who suffer from asthma, eczema and hayfever.

2 Cut the courgettes in half, then into four pieces. Heat the oil in a large frying pan. Add the courgettes to the pan and fry over a medium heat until soft. Remove from the pan. Add the chopped garlic and fry until golden. Stir in the hot chilli sauce.

3 Add the scallops to the sauce. Cook, stirring constantly, for 1–2 minutes only. So not overcook them or they will toughen. Stir in the lime juice, chopped coriander and the courgette pieces. Serve the scallops immediately on heated plates.

COOK'S TIP
Oil can withstand higher temperatures than butter, but butter gives added flavour. Using a mixture of oil and butter provides the perfect compromise.

INGREDIENTS

free from
- ✓ nuts
- ✓ dairy
- ✓ wheat
- seafood
- ✓ eggs
- ✓ yeast
- citrus
- ✓ alcohol

Serves four
20 scallops
2 courgettes (zucchini)
45ml/3 tbsp vegetable oil
4 garlic cloves, chopped
30ml/2 tbsp hot chilli sauce
juice of 1 lime
small bunch of fresh coriander (cilantro), finely chopped

1 If you have bought scallops in their shells, open them. Hold a scallop shell in the palm of your hand, with the flat side uppermost. Insert the blade of a knife close to the hinge that joins the shells and prise them apart. Run the blade of the knife across the inside of the flat shell to cut away the scallop. Only the white adductor muscle and the orange coral are eaten, so pull away and discard all other parts. Rinse the scallops under cold running water.

NUTRITION NOTES

Per portion:

Energy	204Kcal/849kJ
Fat	10g
saturated fat	1.4g
Carbohydrate	3.4g
Fibre	0.9g
Calcium	142.2mg

goan fish casserole

THIS WONDERFULLY FLAVOURED DISH of fish and prawns in a spicy, coconut sauce offers a supply of nutrients that are good for people who have asthma, eczema and hayfever.

INGREDIENTS

Serves four

7.5ml/1½ tsp ground turmeric
5ml/1 tsp salt
450g/1lb monkfish fillet, cut
   into eight pieces
15ml/1 tbsp lemon juice
5ml/1 tsp cumin seeds
5ml/1 tsp coriander seeds
5ml/1 tsp black peppercorns
1 garlic clove, chopped
5cm/2in piece fresh root ginger,
   finely chopped
25g/1oz tamarind paste
150ml/¼ pint/⅔ cup hot water
30ml/2 tbsp vegetable oil
2 onions, halved and sliced lengthways
400ml/14fl oz/1⅔ cups coconut milk
4 mild green chillies, seeded and sliced
16 large raw prawns (shrimp), peeled
30ml/2 tbsp chopped fresh coriander
   (cilantro) leaves, to garnish

3 Preheat the oven to 200°C/400°F/ Gas 6. Mix the tamarind paste with the hot water and set aside.

4 Heat the oil in a frying pan, add the onions and cook for 5–6 minutes, until softened and golden. Transfer the onions to a shallow baking dish.

5 Add the fish fillets to the oil remaining in the frying pan, and fry briefly over a high heat, turning them to seal on all sides. Remove the fish from the pan and place on top of the onions. Add the ground spice mixture to the frying pan and cook over a medium heat, stirring constantly, for 1–2 minutes.

6 Stir in the tamarind liquid, coconut milk and chilli strips and bring to the boil.

7 Pour the sauce into the dish to coat the fish completely, then cover the dish and bake for 10 minutes. Add the prawns, pushing them into the liquid, then cover the dish again and return it to the oven for 5 minutes, or until the prawns turn pink. Do not overcook them. Check the seasoning, sprinkle with coriander leaves and serve.

NUTRITION NOTES

Per portion:

Energy	368Kcal/1538kJ
Fat	23.2g
saturated fat	14.8g
Carbohydrate	14.3g
Fibre	1g
Calcium	119.8mg

1 Mix together the turmeric and salt. Place the monkfish in a dish and sprinkle over the lemon juice, then rub the turmeric and salt mixture over the fish fillets to coat them. Cover and chill until ready to cook.

2 Put the cumin and coriander seeds and black peppercorns in a blender and blend to a powder. Add the garlic and ginger and process for a few seconds more.

free from

✓ nuts
✓ dairy
✓ wheat
  seafood
✓ eggs
✓ yeast
  citrus
✓ alcohol

vegetarian
dishes

From stews and bakes to rice or barley risottos there are main courses here to tempt vegetarians and meat-eaters alike. Choose from classic recipes such as vegetable stew with roasted tomato and garlic sauce, packed with a range of health-giving nutrients, or peppers filled with spiced vegetables, which may help alleviate congestion. Or try something a little more unusual: roasted squash with rice stuffing, which is free from common allergens, or vegetables baked turkish-style, full of vitamin C and betacarotene to ensure a healthy immune system.

peppers filled with spiced vegetables

THE GARLIC, ONION AND FRESH GINGER used in these spicy stuffed peppers may help to alleviate congestion, while the red peppers offer a useful supply of immune-boosting betacarotene.

INGREDIENTS

Serves three as a main course, six as first course

6 large red or yellow (bell) peppers
500g/1¼lb waxy potatoes, scrubbed
1 small onion, chopped
4–5 garlic cloves, chopped
5cm/2in piece fresh root ginger, chopped
1–2 green chillies, seeded and chopped
105ml/7 tbsp water
60ml/4 tbsp olive oil
1 aubergine (eggplant), cut into
   1cm/½in dice
10ml/2 tsp cumin seeds
5ml/1 tsp kalonji seeds
2.5ml/½ tsp ground turmeric
5ml/1 tsp ground coriander
5ml/1 tsp ground toasted cumin seeds
1–2 pinches of cayenne pepper
about 30ml/2 tbsp lemon juice
salt and ground black pepper
30ml/2 tbsp chopped fresh coriander
   (cilantro), to garnish

1 Cut the tops off the red or yellow peppers, then remove and discard the seeds. Cut a thin slice off the base of the peppers, to make them stand upright.

2 Bring a large pan of lightly salted water to the boil. Add the peppers and cook for 5–6 minutes. Drain and leave the peppers upside down in a colander.

3 Cook the potatoes in boiling, salted water for 10–12 minutes, until just tender. Drain, cool and peel, then dice.

4 Purée the onion, garlic, ginger and chillies in a food processor with 60ml/4 tbsp of the water.

5 Heat 30ml/2 tbsp of the oil in a large frying pan and cook the aubergine stirring until browned. Remove and set aside. Add another 15ml/1 tbsp of the oil to the pan and cook the potatoes until lightly browned. Remove and set aside.

6 Add the cumin and kalonji seeds to the pan. Fry briefly, then add the turmeric, coriander and ground cumin. Cook for 15 seconds. Stir in the onion and garlic purée and fry for a few seconds. Return the potatoes and aubergines to the pan, season and add the cayenne.

7 Add the remaining water and 15ml/1 tbsp lemon juice and cook, stirring, until the liquid evaporates. Preheat the oven to 190°C/375°F/Gas 5.

8 Fill the peppers with the mixture and place on a greased baking tray. Brush with a little oil and bake for 30–35 minutes until cooked. Garnish with the chopped coriander and serve.

NUTRITION NOTES

Per portion:	
Energy	434Kcal/1814kJ
Fat	18.4g
saturated fat	2.1g
Carbohydrate	59.9g
Fibre	10.1g
Calcium	145.6mg

roasted squash with rice stuffing

THESE SIMPLE STUFFED VEGETABLES make a light and tasty vegetarian supper. They are free of the common allergens that can exacerbate the symptoms of asthma, eczema and hayfever.

INGREDIENTS

Serves four as a first course

4 whole gem squashes
225g/8oz cooked white long grain rice (about 90g/3½oz/½ cup raw weight)
75g/3oz sun-dried tomatoes in oil, drained and chopped
50g/2oz/½ cup pitted black olives, chopped
30ml/2 tbsp olive oil
15ml/1 tbsp chopped fresh basil leaves, plus basil sprigs to serve
green salad, to serve

1 Preheat the oven to 180°C/350°F/ Gas 4. Using a sharp knife, trim the base of each squash, then slice off the top of each and scoop out and discard the seeds.

2 Mix the rice, tomatoes, olives, half the oil and the chopped basil in a bowl.

3 Oil a shallow baking dish, just large enough to hold the squash side by side, with the remaining oil. Divide the rice mixture among the squash and place them in the baking dish.

4 Cover with foil and bake for about 45 minutes, or until the squash are tender when pierced with the point of a knife or a skewer. Garnish with basil and serve with green salad.

NUTRITION NOTES

Per portion:	
Energy	252Kcal/1058kJ
Fat	10g
saturated fat	1.3g
Carbohydrate	38.5g
Fibre	5g
Calcium	116.6mg

free from
✓ nuts
✓ dairy
✓ wheat
✓ seafood
✓ eggs
✓ yeast
✓ citrus
✓ alcohol

vegetable paella

THIS VEGETARIAN VERSION of the traditional seafood-packed paella is great for anyone who needs to avoid fish and shellfish. Here it is crammed with health-promoting vegetables, including onions and garlic, which are reputed to aid and promote good respiratory function.

INGREDIENTS

Serves four

1 large aubergine (eggplant)
45ml/3 tbsp extra virgin olive oil
2 onions, quartered and sliced
2 garlic cloves, crushed
300g/11oz/1½ cups short grain
   Spanish or risotto rice
1.2–1.5 litres/2–2½ pints/5–6¼ cups
   fresh vegetable stock
1 red (bell) pepper, halved, seeded
   and sliced
200g/7oz fine green beans, halved
115g/4oz/2 cups chestnut mushrooms or
   button (white) mushrooms, halved
1 dried chilli, crushed
115g/4oz/1 cup frozen peas
salt and ground black pepper
fresh coriander (cilantro) leaves, to garnish

1 Soak a Chinese sand pot or clay pot in cold water for 20 minutes, then drain. Cut the aubergine in half lengthwise, then cut it crosswise into thin slices.

VARIATION

Those with an allergy or intolerance to yeast should avoid eating mushrooms, use 115g/4oz carrots instead.

2 Heat 30ml/2 tbsp of the oil in a large frying pan, add the aubergine slices and quickly sauté them until slightly golden. Transfer to the sand pot or clay pot.

3 Add the remaining oil to the pan, add the onion and cook, stirring occasionally, for a 5–10 minutes until softened and golden brown. Add the garlic and rice and cook for 1–2 minutes, stirring, until the rice becomes transparent.

4 Pour in 900ml/1½ pints/3¾ cups of the stock into the sand pot or clay pot, then add the rice mixture.

5 Add the peppers, halved green beans, mushrooms, crushed chilli and seasoning. Stir to mix, then cover the pot and place in an unheated oven.

6 Set the oven to 200°C/400°F/Gas 6 and cook for 1 hour, or until the rice is almost tender. After 40 minutes, remove the pot from the oven and add a little more stock to moisten the paella. Stir well, re-cover and return to the oven.

7 When the paella has cooked for 1 hour, add the peas and a little more stock and stir gently to mix, then return to the oven and cook for a further 10 minutes. Adjust the seasoning and sprinkle over the coriander. Lightly stir through and then serve.

NUTRITION NOTES

Per portion:

Energy	418Kcal/1745kJ
Fat	10.4g
saturated fat	1.5g
Carbohydrate	73.3g
Fibre	7.4g
Calcium	104.8mg

barley risotto with roasted squash and leeks

A HEARTY RISOTTO makes a good choice for those avoiding wheat. Barley contains magnesium, which is thought to be beneficial to sufferers of asthma, eczema and hayfever.

INGREDIENTS

Serves four

200g/7oz/1 cup pearl barley
1 butternut squash, peeled, seeded and
    cut into chunks
10ml/2 tsp chopped fresh thyme
60ml/4 tbsp olive oil
4 leeks, cut into fairly thick diagonal slices
2 garlic cloves, finely chopped
2 carrots, coarsely grated
120ml/4fl oz/½ cup fresh vegetable stock
30ml/2 tbsp chopped fresh flat leaf parsley
50g/2oz Pecorino cheese, grated or
    shaved (optional)
salt and ground black pepper

1 Rinse the barley. Cook it in simmering water, keeping the pan part-covered, for 35–45 minutes. Drain. Preheat the oven to 200°C/400°F/Gas 6.

free from
- ✓ nuts
- dairy
- ✓ wheat
- ✓ seafood
- ✓ eggs
- yeast
- ✓ citrus
- ✓ alcohol

2 Place the squash in a roasting pan with half the thyme. Season with pepper and toss with half the oil. Roast, stirring once, for 30–35 minutes until tender.

3 Heat the remaining oil in a large frying pan. Cook the leeks and garlic gently for 5 minutes.

4 Add the remaining thyme, then cook for 3 minutes. Stir in the carrots, cook for 2 minutes, then add the barley and most of the stock. Season well and part-cover the pan. Cook for 5 minutes more. Pour in the remaining stock if the mixture seems dry.

5 Stir in the parsley and half the Pecorino, if using, then stir in the squash. Add seasoning to taste and serve with the remaining Pecorino.

NUTRITION NOTES

Per portion:

Energy	396Kcal/1666kJ
Fat	13.1g
saturated fat	1.7g
Carbohydrate	64.7g
Fibre	7.6g
Calcium	165mg

rice and lentils with crisp caramelized onions

THE ONIONS IN THIS DISH offer anti-inflammatory properties for asthma sufferers, while lentils and rice are a good carbohydrate choice for those who suffer from wheat allergies.

INGREDIENTS

Serves six

400g/14oz/1¾ cups large brown or
    green lentils
30ml/2 tbsp olive oil
3–4 onions, 1 chopped and
    2–3 thinly sliced
5ml/1 tsp ground cumin
2.5ml/½ tsp ground cinnamon
3–5 cardamom pods
300g/11oz/1½ cups long grain
    rice, rinsed
250ml/8fl oz/1 cup fresh vegetable stock
salt and ground black pepper
natural (plain) yogurt, to serve (optional)

1 Put the lentils in a large pan with enough water to cover generously. Bring to the boil, then reduce the heat and simmer for about 30 minutes, or until the lentils are just tender. Once or twice during cooking, skim off any scum that forms on top.

2 Heat half the olive oil in a small pan, add the chopped onion and fry for 5 minutes, stirring frequently or until the onion is starting to turn golden brown. Stir in half the ground cumin and half the ground cinnamon.

3 Heat the remaining oil in a frying pan, add the sliced onions and fry for 10 minutes, until brown and crisp. Sprinkle in the remaining cumin and cinnamon.

4 Add the fried chopped onion to the lentils with the cardamom, rice and stock.

5 Mix, then bring to the boil. Reduce the heat, cover and simmer until the rice is tender and the liquid has been absorbed. Season. To serve, pile the rice and lentil mixture on to a warmed serving dish, then top with the caramelized onions. Serve with natural yogurt, if you like.

NUTRITION NOTES

Per portion:

Energy	449Kcal/1903kJ
Fat	5.8g
saturated fat	0.6g
Carbohydrate	83.5g
Fibre	7.1g
Calcium	91.4mg

free from
✓ nuts
  dairy
✓ wheat
✓ seafood
✓ eggs
✓ yeast
✓ citrus
✓ alcohol

vegetable stew with roasted tomato and garlic sauce

A TASTY STEW PACKED with fresh vegetables that offers a valuable supply of health-promoting nutrients. If you are on a yeast-free diet, simply omit the dried apricots.

INGREDIENTS

Serves six

45ml/3 tbsp olive oil
250g/9oz small pickling onions
  or shallots
1 large onion, chopped
2 garlic cloves, chopped
5ml/1 tsp cumin seeds
5ml/1 tsp ground coriander seeds
5ml/1 tsp paprika
5cm/2in piece cinnamon stick
2 fresh bay leaves
300–450ml/½–¾ pint/1¼–scant 2 cups
  fresh vegetable stock
good pinch of saffron strands
450g/1lb carrots, thickly sliced
2 green (bell) peppers, seeded and
  thickly sliced
115g/4oz ready-to-eat dried apricots
5ml/1 tsp ground toasted cumin seeds
450g/1lb squash, peeled, seeded and
  cut into chunks
pinch of sugar, to taste
salt and ground black pepper
45ml/3 tbsp fresh coriander (cilantro)
  leaves, to garnish

**For the roasted tomato
and garlic sauce**

1kg/2¼lb tomatoes, halved
45ml/3 tbsp olive oil
1–2 fresh red chillies, seeded
  and chopped
2–3 garlic cloves, chopped
5ml/1 tsp fresh thyme leaves

1 Preheat the oven to 180°C/350°F/ Gas 4. First make the sauce. Place the tomatoes, cut sides uppermost, in a roasting tin. Season well, then drizzle with the olive oil. Roast for 30 minutes.

2 Scatter the chillies, garlic and thyme over the tomatoes, stir to mix and roast for another 30–45 minutes, or until the tomatoes are collapsed but still a little juicy. Leave the tomatoes to cool, then process in a food processor or blender to make a thick sauce. Sieve to remove the seeds.

3 Heat 30ml/2 tbsp of the olive oil in a large, wide pan or deep frying pan and cook the pickling onions or shallots until browned all over. Remove them from the pan and set aside. Add the chopped onion to the pan and cook over a low heat for 5–7 minutes until softened. Stir in the chopped garlic and cumin seeds and cook for a further 3–4 minutes.

4 Add the ground coriander seeds, paprika, cinnamon stick and bay leaves. Cook, stirring constantly, for another 2 minutes, then mix in the stock, saffron, carrots and green peppers. Season well, cover and simmer gently for 10 minutes.

5 Stir in the apricots, ground cumin, browned onions or shallots and squash. Stir in the tomato sauce. Cover and cook for 5 minutes more. Uncover the pan and cook, stirring occasionally, for 10–15 minutes, until the vegetables are cooked.

6 Add sugar to taste, adjust the seasoning, then discard the cinnamon stick. Serve scattered with the fresh coriander leaves.

NUTRITION NOTES

Per portion:

Energy	173Kcal/721kJ
Fat	6.8g
saturated fat	0.8g
Carbohydrate	25.2g
Fibre	5.9g
Calcium	120mg

vegetables baked turkish-style

THIS SPICY VEGETABLE STEW is packed with healthy non-allergenic vegetables, which are rich in nutrients such as vitamin C and betacarotene.

INGREDIENTS

Serves four

60ml/4 tbsp olive oil

1 large onion, chopped

2 aubergines (eggplant), cut into small cubes

4 courgettes (zucchini), cut into small chunks

1 green (bell) pepper, seeded and chopped

1 red or yellow (bell) pepper, seeded and chopped

115g/4oz/1 cup fresh or frozen peas

115g/4oz green beans

450g/1lb small new or salad potatoes, cubed

2.5ml/½ tsp ground cinnamon

2.5ml/½ tsp ground cumin

5ml/1 tsp paprika

4–5 tomatoes, skinned

400g/14oz can chopped tomatoes

30ml/2 tbsp chopped fresh flat leaf parsley

3–4 garlic cloves, crushed

350ml/12fl oz/1½ cups fresh vegetable stock

salt and ground black pepper

black olives and fresh parsley, to garnish

free from

✓ nuts
✓ dairy
✓ wheat
✓ seafood
✓ eggs
✓ yeast
✓ citrus
✓ alcohol

1 Preheat the oven to 190°C/375°F/ Gas 5. Heat 45ml/3 tbsp of the oil in a large frying pan, add the onion and fry until golden.

2 Add the aubergine cubes and sauté for about 3 minutes, then add the courgette chunks, chopped green and red or yellow peppers, peas, green beans and cubed potatoes, together with the ground cinnamon, ground cumin, paprika and seasoning. Continue to cook for a further 3 minutes, stirring the mixture constantly. Transfer the vegetables to an ovenproof dish.

3 Halve the fresh skinned tomatoes, remove the seeds using a teaspoon and then roughly chop the tomato flesh. Mix the fresh tomato flesh with the canned tomatoes, chopped fresh parsley, crushed garlic and the remaining olive oil in a mixing bowl.

4 Pour the vegetable stock over the aubergine and pepper mixture and then spoon the prepared tomato mixture evenly over the top. Cover the dish with foil and bake for 30–45 minutes. Serve hot, garnished with olives and parsley.

NUTRITION NOTES

Per portion:

Energy	336Kcal/1401kJ
Fat	14.3g
saturated fat	1.9g
Carbohydrate	42.5g
Fibre	10.9g
Calcium	144.3mg

spicy tomato and chickpea stew

TOMATOES OFFER a good supply of anti-inflammatory vitamin C, which can help asthma sufferers. Serve this healthy stew with flatbread or, for those with a wheat allergy, brown rice.

INGREDIENTS

Serves four

60ml/4 tbsp olive oil

1 large aubergine (eggplant), cut into bitesize chunks

2 onions, thinly sliced

3–5 garlic cloves, chopped

1–2 green (bell) peppers, thinly sliced

1–2 fresh hot chillies, chopped

4 fresh or canned tomatoes, diced

30–45ml/2–3 tbsp tomato purée (paste), if using fresh tomatoes

5ml/1 tsp ground turmeric

pinch of curry powder or ras el hanout

cayenne pepper, to taste

400g/14oz can chickpeas, drained and rinsed

30–45ml/2–3 tbsp chopped fresh coriander (cilantro) leaves

salt

flatbread or brown rice, to serve

1 Heat half the oil in a frying pan, add the aubergine chunks and fry until brown. When cooked, transfer the aubergine to a colander, standing over a bowl, and leave to drain.

2 Heat the remaining oil in the pan, add the onions, garlic, peppers and chillies and fry until softened. Add the diced tomatoes, tomato purée, if using, spices and salt, and cook, stirring, until the mixture is of a sauce consistency. Add a little water if necessary.

3 Add the drained and rinsed chickpeas to the sauce and cook for about 5 minutes, then add the browned aubergine, stir thoroughly to mix and cook for 5–10 minutes until the flavours are well combined. Add the chopped coriander leaves. Serve the stew hot or chill before serving.

VARIATION

This stew would be equally good with other vegetables. Try courgettes (zucchini) in place of some or all of the aubergine, or add chunks of squash, sweet potato or carrot.

NUTRITION NOTES

Per portion:

Energy	243Kcal/1012kJ
Fat	13.9g
saturated fat	1.6g
Carbohydrate	23.2g
Fibre	7.2g
Calcium	76.1mg

free from

✓ nuts

✓ dairy

wheat

✓ seafood

✓ eggs

yeast

✓ citrus

✓ alcohol

mixed bean and aubergine tagine

BEANS ARE A GOOD SOURCE of B vitamins, which can help to maintain healthy skin, and onions and garlic are both recommended for respiratory problems. Garlic can also act as a natural decongestant, which can benefit hayfever sufferers.

INGREDIENTS
Serves four

115g/4oz/generous ½ cup dried red
   kidney beans, soaked overnight in cold
   water and drained
115g/4oz/generous ½ cup dried
   black-eyed beans (peas), soaked
   overnight in cold water and drained
600ml/1 pint/2½ cups water
2 bay leaves
2 celery sticks, each cut into four batons
75ml/5 tbsp olive oil
1 aubergine (eggplant), cut into chunks
1 onion, thinly sliced
3 garlic cloves, crushed
1–2 fresh red chillies, seeded and chopped
30ml/2 tbsp tomato purée (paste)
5ml/1 tsp paprika
2 large tomatoes, roughly chopped
300ml/½ pint/1¼ cups fresh stock
15ml/1 tbsp each chopped fresh mint,
   parsley and coriander (cilantro)
salt and ground black pepper
fresh herb sprigs, to garnish

free from
- ✓ nuts
- ✓ dairy
- ✓ wheat
- ✓ seafood
- ✓ eggs
- ✓ yeast
- ✓ citrus
- ✓ alcohol

1 Place the kidney beans in a large pan of unsalted boiling water. Bring back to the boil and boil rapidly for 10 minutes, then drain. Place the black-eyed beans in a separate large pan of boiling unsalted water and boil rapidly for 10 minutes, then drain.

2 Place the 600ml/1 pint/2½ cups of water in a soaked bean pot or a large tagine, add the bay leaves, celery and beans. Cover and place in an unheated oven. Set the oven to 190°C/375°F/Gas 5. Cook for 1–1½ hours, or until the beans are tender. Drain.

3 Heat 60ml/4 tbsp of the oil in a large frying pan. Add the aubergine and cook, stirring for 4–5 minutes until evenly browned. Remove and set aside.

4 Add the remaining oil to the frying pan, then add the onion and cook, stirring, for 4–5 minutes until softened. Add the garlic and chillies and cook for a further 5 minutes, stirring frequently, until the onion is golden.

5 Reduce the oven temperature to 160°C/325°F/Gas 3. Add the tomato purée and paprika to the pan and cook, stirring, for 1–2 minutes. Add the chopped tomatoes, browned aubergine, drained kidney and black-eyed beans and stock. Stir well, then season to taste with salt and pepper.

6 Transfer the contents of the frying pan to a soaked clay tagine or a shallow baking dish. Place in the oven and cook for 1 hour, or until the vegetables are tender.

7 To serve, add the chopped mint, parsley and coriander to the tagine and lightly mix through the vegetables. Season to taste with salt and plenty of pepper. Garnish with fresh herb sprigs and serve.

NUTRITION NOTES

Per portion:	
Energy	334Kcal/1401kJ
Fat	15.5g
saturated fat	2.1g
Carbohydrate	35.5g
Fibre	12.6g
Calcium	139.6mg

salads and side dishes

It's so easy to stick with the old favourites when it comes to main course or side salads and accompanying vegetable dishes, but try just one of these alternatives and you'll soon be converted to serving vegetables with a twist. Try salads such as beetroot with fresh mint, a wonderfully colourful dish with immune-boosting betacarotene or beef and grilled sweet potato salad with shallot and herb dressing that has anti-viral properties. Accompanying vegetable dishes include spinach with raisins and pine nuts (a good source of vitamin C) and oven-roasted red onions with natural anti-inflammatory properties.

beetroot with fresh mint

THIS REFRESHING SALAD is a tasty way to serve beetroot. Avoid the pickled variety, as it is loaded with histamines and may aggravate allergies.

INGREDIENTS

Serves four

4 large or 6–8 large cooked
   beetroot (beets)
5–10ml/1–2 tsp sugar
juice of ½ lemon
30ml/2 tbsp extra virgin olive oil
1 bunch fresh mint, leaves stripped and
   thinly sliced

COOK'S TIP

If you are going to buy ready-cooked beetroot for this salad, ensure that it is not the pickled variety. If you prefer to cook it yourself, simmer the unskinned beetroot for about 1½ hours.

1 Slice the beetroot or cut into even-size dice with a sharp knife. Put the beetroot in a bowl. Add the sugar, lemon juice, olive oil and a pinch of salt and toss together to combine.

2 Add half the thinly sliced fresh mint to the salad and toss lightly until well combined. Place the salad in the refrigerator and chill for about 1 hour. Serve garnished with the remaining mint.

NUTRITION NOTES

Per portion:

Energy	79Kcal/327kJ
Fat	5.6g
saturated fat	0.8g
Carbohydrate	6.3g
Fibre	1g
Calcium	20.1mg

free from

✓ nuts
✓ dairy
✓ wheat
✓ seafood
✓ eggs
✓ yeast
  citrus
✓ alcohol

carrot salad

THIS TASTY SALAD is rich in health-promoting nutrients including betacarotene and vitamin C. The generous quantities of garlic can act as a decongestant and provides anti-viral properties.

INGREDIENTS

Serves four

3–4 carrots, thinly sliced
5ml/1 tsp sugar
3–4 garlic cloves, chopped
1.5ml/¼ tsp ground cumin,
 or to taste
juice of ½ lemon
30–45ml/2–3 tbsp extra virgin
 olive oil
30ml/2 tbsp chopped fresh coriander
 (cilantro) leaves or a mixture of
 coriander and flat leaf parsley
salt and ground black pepper

1 Cook the carrots by either steaming or boiling in lightly salted water until they are just tender but not soft. Drain, leave for a few moments to dry, then put in a bowl.

2 Add the sugar, garlic, cumin, lemon juice and olive oil to the carrots and toss together. Add the herbs and season. Serve warm or chill before serving.

NUTRITION NOTES

Per portion:

Energy	97Kcal/401kJ
Fat	5.9g
saturated fat	0.8g
Carbohydrate	10.3g
Fibre	2.6g
Calcium	35.7mg

free from

✓ nuts
✓ dairy
✓ wheat
✓ seafood
✓ eggs
✓ yeast
  citrus
✓ alcohol

bean salad with tuna and red onion

THE ESSENTIAL FATTY ACIDS found in tuna fish and B vitamins found in beans may help to improve the skin of eczema sufferers.

2 Place all the dressing ingredients apart from the lemon juice in a jug (pitcher) and whisk until mixed. Season to taste with salt, pepper and lemon juice, if you like.

3 Blanch the French beans in boiling water for 3–4 minutes. Drain, refresh under cold water and drain again.

4 Place both types of beans in a bowl. Add half the dressing and toss to mix. Stir in the onion and half the parsley, then season to taste with salt and pepper. Flake the tuna into large chunks and lightly toss it into the beans with the tomatoes.

5 Arrange the salad on four plates. Drizzle the remaining dressing over and scatter the remaining parsley on top.

INGREDIENTS

Serves four

250g/9oz/1⅓ cups dried haricot or cannellini beans, soaked overnight in cold water
1 bay leaf
200–250g/7–9oz fine French beans, trimmed
1 large red onion, very thinly sliced
45ml/3 tbsp chopped fresh flat leaf parsley
200–250g/7–9oz good-quality canned tuna in olive oil, drained
200g/7oz cherry tomatoes, halved
salt and ground black pepper

For the dressing

90ml/6 tbsp extra virgin olive oil
5ml/1 tsp tarragon mustard
1 garlic clove, finely chopped
5ml/1 tsp grated lemon rind
a little lemon juice

1 Drain the beans and place them in a large pan with fresh water. Add the bay leaf, then bring to the boil. Boil rapidly for 10 minutes, then reduce the heat and boil steadily for 1–1½ hours until tender. The cooking time depends on the age of the beans. Drain well. Discard the bay leaf.

free from
✓ nuts
✓ dairy
✓ wheat
  seafood
✓ eggs
  yeast
  citrus
  alcohol

NUTRITION NOTES

Per portion:

Energy	445Kcal/1864kJ
Fat	21.9g
saturated fat	3.1g
Carbohydrate	37.8g
Fibre	13.2g
Calcium	168.8mg

lentil and spinach salad

A HEALTHY SALAD packed with nutrients that will help to keep the body in peak condition, boost the immune system and promote good skin health.

INGREDIENTS

Serves six

225g/8oz/1 cup Puy lentils
1 fresh bay leaf
1 celery stick
fresh thyme sprig
30ml/2 tbsp olive oil
1 onion or 3–4 shallots, finely chopped
10ml/2 tsp crushed toasted cumin seeds
400g/14oz young spinach
salt and ground black pepper
30–45ml/2–3 tbsp chopped fresh parsley
toasted French bread, to serve (optional)

For the dressing

75ml/5 tbsp extra virgin olive oil
5ml/1 tsp Dijon mustard
1 small garlic clove, finely chopped
15ml/1 tbsp lemon juice, plus 2.5ml/
½ tsp finely grated lemon rind

1 Rinse the lentils and place them in a large saucepan. Add plenty of water to cover. Tie the bay leaf, celery and thyme into a bundle and add to the pan, then bring to the boil. Reduce the heat so that the water boils steadily. Cook the lentils for 30–45 minutes until just tender. Do not add salt at this stage, as it toughens the lentils.

2 Meanwhile, to make the dressing, mix the oil, mustard, garlic and lemon juice and rind, and season well.

3 Thoroughly drain the lentils and tip them into a bowl. Add most of the dressing and toss well, then set the lentils aside, stirring occasionally.

4 Heat the oil in a deep frying pan and cook the onion or shallots over a low heat for about 4–5 minutes until they are beginning to soften. Add the cumin and cook for 1 minute. Add the spinach and season to taste, cover and cook for 2 minutes. Stir, then cook again briefly until wilted.

5 Stir the lightly cooked spinach into the lentils and then leave the salad to cool, then chill until ready to serve. Bring back to room temperature if necessary. Stir in the remaining dressing and chopped parsley.

6 Adjust the seasoning, adding plenty of black pepper, then tip the salad on to a serving dish or into a large salad bowl and serve with toasted French bread, if you like.

NUTRITION NOTES

Per portion:	
Energy	177Kcal/746kJ
Fat	5.3g
saturated fat	0.6g
Carbohydrate	21.9g
Fibre	5.3g
Calcium	173.6mg

free from
✓ nuts
✓ dairy
wheat
✓ seafood
✓ eggs
yeast
citrus
alcohol

spicy white bean salad

TENDER WHITE BEANS, a good source of B vitamins, are delicious in this spicy sauce with the bite of fresh, crunchy green pepper. The dish is perfect for preparing ahead of time.

INGREDIENTS

Serves four

750g/1⅔lb tomatoes, diced
1 onion, finely chopped
½–1 mild fresh chilli, finely chopped
1 green (bell) pepper, seeded and
  chopped
pinch of sugar
4 garlic cloves, chopped
400g/14oz can cannellini beans, drained
45–60ml/3–4 tbsp olive oil
grated rind and juice of 1 lemon
15ml/1 tbsp cider vinegar or
  wine vinegar
salt and ground black pepper
chopped fresh parsley, to garnish

1 Put the tomatoes, onion, chilli, green pepper, sugar, garlic, cannellini beans, salt and plenty of ground black pepper in a bowl and toss together until well combined.

2 Add the olive oil, grated lemon rind, lemon juice and vinegar to the salad and toss lightly to combine. Chill before serving, garnished with chopped parsley.

NUTRITION NOTES

Per portion:

Energy	195Kcal/1810kJ
Fat	9.6g
saturated fat	1.3g
Carbohydrate	21.5g
Fibre	6.2g
Calcium	63.8mg

free from

✓	nuts
✓	dairy
✓	wheat
✓	seafood
✓	eggs
	yeast
	citrus
	alcohol

beef and grilled sweet potato salad

A SOPHISTICATED SALAD that makes a delicious low-allergy lunch or supper. Sweet potato contains immune-boosting betacarotene and shallots may act as a decongestant.

INGREDIENTS

Serves six

800g/1¾lb fillet steak (beef tenderloin)
5ml/1 tsp black peppercorns,
  coarsely crushed
10ml/2 tsp chopped fresh thyme
45ml/3 tbsp olive oil
450g/1lb orange-fleshed sweet
  potato, peeled
salt and ground black pepper

For the dressing

1 garlic clove, chopped
15g/½oz flat leaf parsley
30ml/2 tbsp chopped fresh
  coriander (cilantro)
½–1 fresh green chilli, seeded
  and chopped
10ml/2 tsp Dijon mustard
45ml/3 tbsp extra virgin olive oil
2 shallots, finely chopped

1 Roll the beef fillet in the coarsely crushed peppercorns and thyme, then set aside to marinate for a few hours.

2 Preheat the oven to 200°C/400°F/ Gas 6. Heat half the olive oil in a heavy frying pan. Add the beef and brown it all over, turning frequently, to seal it.

3 Place on a baking tray and cook in the oven for 10–15 minutes. Remove the beef from the oven, and cover with foil, then leave to rest for 10–15 minutes.

4 Meanwhile, preheat the grill. Cut the sweet potatoes into 1cm/½in slices. Brush with the remaining olive oil, season to taste with salt and pepper, and grill for about 5–6 minutes on each side, until tender and browned. Cut the sweet potato slices into strips and place them in a bowl. Cut the beef into strips and toss with the sweet potato. Set the bowl aside.

5 To make the dressing, process the garlic, parsley, coriander, chilli and mustard in a food processor or blender until chopped. With the motor still running, gradually pour in the oil to make a smooth dressing. Season, then stir in the shallots.

6 Toss the dressing into the sweet potatoes and beef and leave to stand in a cool place for up to 2 hours before serving.

VARIATION

Skinless, boneless chicken breasts would make a lower-fat alternative to beef in this salad – ensure that it is cooked right through.

NUTRITION NOTES

Per portion:

Energy	350Kcal/1457kJ
Fat	19.6g
saturated fat	5g
Carbohydrate	14.8g
Fibre	1.7g
Calcium	41.5mg

free from

✓ nuts
✓ dairy
✓ wheat
✓ seafood
✓ eggs
  yeast
✓ citrus
  alcohol

spinach with raisins and pine nuts

AN ENERGIZING SIDE DISH that aids the elimination of toxins and enhances immunity, helping the body fight off infection. Those with a nut allergy should simply omit the pine nuts.

INGREDIENTS

Serves four
60ml/4 tbsp raisins
1kg/2¼lb fresh spinach leaves, washed
45ml/3 tbsp olive oil
6–8 spring onions (scallions), thinly sliced
  or 1–2 small yellow or white onions,
  finely chopped
60ml/4 tbsp pine nuts (optional)
salt and ground black pepper

1 Put the raisins in a small bowl and pour over boiling water to cover. Leave to stand for about 10 minutes, then drain.

2 Steam the spinach over a medium-high heat, with only the water that clings to it after washing, for 1–2 minutes until the leaves are bright green and wilted. Drain well leave to cool. When the spinach has cooled, chop roughly with a sharp knife.

3 Heat the oil in a frying pan over a medium-low heat, then lower the heat a little and add the sliced spring onions or onions. Fry for about 5 minutes, stirring occasionally, or until soft, then add the spinach, raisins and pine nuts, if using.

4 Raise the heat a little and then cook the spinach mixture for 2–3 minutes to warm through. Season with salt and plenty of pepper to taste and serve hot or warm.

NUTRITION NOTES

Per portion:
Energy	195Kcal/810kJ
Fat	10.4g
saturated fat	1.6g
Carbohydrate	18.4g
Fibre	5.8g
Calcium	440.2mg

free from
	nuts
✓	dairy
✓	wheat
✓	seafood
✓	eggs
	yeast
✓	citrus
✓	alcohol

baked winter squash in tomato sauce

THIS HEALTHY ANTI-ASTHMA SIDE DISH contains immune-boosting betacarotene, health-promoting and histamine-fighting vitamin C, and anti-inflammatory onions.

INGREDIENTS

Serves four

45–75ml/3–5 tbsp olive oil
1kg/2¼lb pumpkin or orange winter
   squash, peeled and sliced
1 onion, chopped
1–2 garlic cloves, chopped
2 x 400g/14oz cans chopped tomatoes
pinch of sugar
2–3 sprigs of fresh rosemary, stems
   removed and leaves chopped
salt and ground black pepper

1 Preheat the oven to 160°C/325°F/ Gas 3. Heat 45ml/3 tbsp of the oil in a frying pan and fry the pumpkin or orange squash slices in batches until golden brown on all sides. Remove the pumpkin or orange squash slices from the pan as they are cooked and keep warm.

2 Add the onion to the pan, with more oil if necessary, and fry for about 5 minutes, stirring, until softened.

3 Add the garlic to the pan and cook for 1 minute, stirring all the time, then add the tomatoes and sugar and cook over a medium-high heat, stirring occasionally, until the mixture is of a thick sauce consistency. Stir in the chopped rosemary leaves and season with salt and and plenty of pepper to taste.

4 Layer the fried pumpkin or squash slices and the tomato sauce in a shallow ovenproof dish, ending with a layer of tomato sauce.

5 Transfer the dish to the oven and bake for about 35 minutes, or until the top layer of sauce is lightly glazed and the pumpkin or squash is tender and just beginning to turn a light golden brown. Serve immediately.

NUTRITION NOTES

Per portion:	
Energy	143Kcal/595kJ
Fat	8.9g
saturated fat	1.2g
Carbohydrate	12.4g
Fibre	4.2g
Calcium	78.8,g

free from
✓ nuts
✓ dairy
✓ wheat
✓ seafood
✓ eggs
✓ yeast
✓ citrus
✓ alcohol

oven-roasted red onions

SWEET RED ONIONS are the perfect side dish for those striving to combat the symptoms of asthma. Onions have natural anti-inflammatory properties, which can help to calm an irritated respiratory system.

3 Rub the onions with half the olive oil, salt and pepper and the juniper berries. Place the onions in the baker, inserting the rosemary in among the onions. Pour the remaining olive oil over.

4 Cover and place in an unheated oven. Set the oven to 200°C/400°F/Gas 6 and cook for 40 minutes. Remove the lid and cook for a further 10 minutes until the onions are tender and the skins slightly crisp.

COOK'S TIP

To help hold back the tears during preparation, chill the onions first for about 30 minutes and then remove the root end last. The root contains the largest concentration of the sulphuric compounds that make the eyes water.

INGREDIENTS

Serves four

4 large or 8 small red onions
45ml/3 tbsp olive oil
6 juniper berries, crushed
8 small sprigs of fresh rosemary
salt and ground black pepper

free from

✓ nuts
✓ dairy
✓ wheat
✓ seafood
✓ eggs
✓ yeast
✓ citrus
✓ alcohol

1 Soak a clay onion baker in cold water for 15 minutes, then drain. If the base of the baker is glazed, only the lid will need to be soaked.

VARIATION

If you like, try using just fresh thyme in place of the juniper and rosemary.

2 Trim the roots from the onions and remove the skins, if you like. Cut the onions from the tip to the root, cutting the large onions into quarters and the small onions in half.

NUTRITION NOTES

Per portion:

Energy	141Kcal/583kJ
Fat	8.7g
saturated fat	1.2g
Carbohydrate	14.5g
Fibre	2.5g
Calcium	49.8mg

braised red cabbage with beetroot

CABBAGE AND, TO A LESSER EXTENT, BEETROOT, are excellent sources of vitamin C, which can help to promote the immune system and eliminate histamines that are produced during an allergic reaction.

INGREDIENTS

Serves six

675g/1½lb red cabbage
30ml/2 tbsp olive oil
1 Spanish onion, thinly sliced into rings
2 tart eating apples, peeled, cored and sliced
300ml/½ pint/1¼ cups fresh vegetable stock
375g/13oz raw beetroot (beet), peeled and coarsely grated
salt and ground black pepper

1 Soak a large clay pot or bean pot in cold water for 20 minutes, then drain. Finely shred the red cabbage and place in the soaked clay or bean pot.

2 Heat the olive oil in a large frying pan, add the thinly sliced Spanish onion and cook gently for about 5 minutes, stirring occasionally, until the onion is soft and transparent.

COOK'S TIP
When buying cabbage, choose one that is firm and heavy for its size. The leaves should look healthy – avoid any with curling leaves or blemishes. These guidelines apply to any type of cabbage – red, green or white.

3 Add the apple slices to the pan and pour in the vegetable stock, then transfer the mixture to the clay or bean pot. Season with salt and plenty of pepper and stir well to combine the sliced apple, onion and cabbage.

4 Cover the clay or bean pot and place in an unheated oven. Set the oven temperature to 190°C/375°F/Gas 5 and cook for about 1 hour. Stir in the beetroot, then re-cover the pot and cook for 20–30 minutes, or until tender.

NUTRITION NOTES

Per portion:

Energy	111Kcal/463kJ
Fat	4.2g
saturated fat	0.5g
Carbohydrate	16.3g
Fibre	5.1g
Calcium	97.4mg

free from
✓ nuts
✓ dairy
✓ wheat
✓ seafood
✓ eggs
✓ yeast
✓ citrus
✓ alcohol

potatoes baked with fennel and onions

VEGETABLES FLAVOURED WITH aromatic spices make a perfect accompaniment to grilled or roasted meat.

INGREDIENTS

Serves six

500g/1¼lb small waxy potatoes, cut into chunks or wedges
good pinch of saffron threads
1 head of garlic, separated into cloves
12 small red or yellow onions, peeled
3 fennel bulbs, cut into wedges, feathery tops reserved
4–6 fresh bay leaves
6–9 fresh thyme sprigs
175ml/6fl oz/¾ cup fresh vegetable stock
5ml/1 tsp fennel seeds, lightly crushed
2.5ml/½ tsp paprika
45ml/3 tbsp olive oil
salt and ground black pepper

1 Boil the potatoes in salted water for 8–10 minutes. Drain. Preheat the oven to 190°C/375°F/Gas 5. Soak the saffron in 30ml/2 tbsp warm water for 10 minutes.

2 Peel and finely chop 2 of the garlic cloves and set them aside. Place the potatoes, onions, unpeeled garlic cloves, fennel wedges, bay leaves and thyme sprigs in a roasting dish.

COOK'S TIP
Don't worry about the amount of garlic in this dish – it becomes very mellow after cooking.

3 Mix together the stock, saffron and its soaking liquid, then pour over the vegetables. Stir in the fennel seeds, paprika, chopped garlic and oil, and season with salt and pepper.

4 Cook in the oven for 1–1¼ hours, stirring occasionally, until the vegetables are tender. Chop the reserved feathery fennel tops and sprinkle over the vegetables and serve.

NUTRITION NOTES

Per portion:

Energy	167Kcal/699kJ
Fat	6.2g
saturated fat	0.8g
Carbohydrate	25g
Fibre	4.1g
Calcium	63.4mg

rice with dill and broad beans

THIS FIBRE-RICH SIDE DISH makes a good accompaniment to any low-allergy main dish.

INGREDIENTS

Serves four

275g/10oz/1½ cups basmati or long grain rice, soaked in cold water and drained

750ml/1¼ pints/3 cups water

45ml/3 tbsp olive oil

175g/6oz/1½ cups frozen baby broad (fava) beans, thawed and peeled

90ml/6 tbsp finely chopped fresh dill, plus fresh dill sprigs to garnish

5ml/1 tsp ground cinnamon

5ml/1 tsp ground cumin

2–3 saffron threads, soaked in 15ml/ 1 tbsp boiling water

1 Tip the soaked and drained rice into a large pan with the water. Add a little salt. Bring to the boil, then simmer very gently for 5 minutes. Drain, rinse in warm water and drain again

2 Pour 15ml/1 tbsp of the oil into the rinsed-out pan. Spoon enough rice into the pan to cover the base. Add one-quarter of the beans and a little dill.

3 Spread over another layer of rice, then a layer of beans and dill. Repeat the layers until all the beans and dill have been used, ending with a layer of rice. Cook over a gentle heat for 8 minutes, without stirring, until nearly tender.

4 Pour the remaining oil evenly over the rice, then sprinkle the ground cinnamon and cumin over the top. Cover the pan with a clean dishtowel or cloth and a tight-fitting lid, lifting the corners of the towel or cloth back over the lid. Cook over a low heat for 25–30 minutes.

5 Spoon about 45ml/3 tbsp of the cooked rice into the bowl of saffron water and then mix the rice and liquid together. Spoon the remaining rice mixture on to a large serving plate and spoon the saffron rice on one side to garnish. Serve immediately, decorated with fresh sprigs of dill.

NUTRITION NOTES

Per portion:	
Energy	368Kcal/1531kJ
Fat	12.4g
saturated fat	11.6g
Carbohydrate	59.5g
Fibre	3.4g
Calcium	98.1mg

free from
- ✓ nuts
- ✓ dairy
- ✓ wheat
- ✓ seafood
- ✓ eggs
- ✓ yeast
- ✓ citrus
- ✓ alcohol

desserts

Eating to beat an allergy doesn't mean you have to miss out on dessert. If you fancy something a little indulgent then choose rich and creamy coconut ice cream – ideal if you have an allergy to dairy products – or deliciously aromatic figs and pears in honey, which is rich in vitamin C. If you prefer a refreshing, fruity dessert then go for gooseberry and elderflower sorbet with a subtle floral hint – it is the ideal choice for asthma and eczema sufferers – or try simple to prepare melon salad with sweet ginger syrup, a light fruit salad with ginger that has decongestive properties.

tropical scented red and orange fruit salad

A COLOURFUL FRESH FRUIT SALAD rich in vitamin C, which can be beneficial for sufferers of asthma, eczema and hayfever because of its anti-inflammatory properties.

INGREDIENTS

Serves four

350–400g/12–14oz/3–3½ cups strawberries, hulled and halved

3 oranges, peeled and segmented

3 blood oranges, peeled and segmented

1–2 passion fruit

120ml/4fl oz/½ cup freshly squeezed orange juice

sugar to taste

free from

✓ nuts
✓ dairy
✓ wheat
✓ seafood
✓ eggs
✓ yeast
 citrus
✓ alcohol

VARIATION

Other fruit that can be added include pear, kiwi fruit and banana.

1 Put the strawberries and oranges into a serving bowl. Halve the passion fruit and spoon the flesh into the fruit.

2 Pour the orange juice over the fruit and add sugar to taste. Toss gently and then chill until ready to serve.

NUTRITION NOTES

Per portion:

Energy	127Kcal/532kJ
Fat	0.4g
saturated fat	0g
Carbohydrate	29.5g
Fibre	4.8g
Calcium	114.4mg

melon salad
with sweet ginger syrup

THIS LIGHT AND REFRESHING FRUIT SALAD is a good source of vitamin C and betacarotene. Ginger is reputed to have decongestive properties.

INGREDIENTS

Serves four

¼ watermelon
½ honeydew melon
½ Charentais melon
60ml/4 tbsp syrup from a jar of preserved
   stem ginger

COOK'S TIPS

- For an even prettier effect, scoop the melon flesh into balls with the large end of a melon baller.
- Make sure the melons are ripe – they should have a strong scent.

1 Remove the seeds from the melons, cut them into wedges, then slice off the rind.

2 Cut all the flesh into chunks and mix in a bowl. Stir in the ginger syrup, cover and chill until ready to serve.

NUTRITION NOTES

Per portion:	
Energy	111Kcal/469kJ
Fat	0.4g
saturated fat	0g
Carbohydrate	27.4g
Fibre	0.8g
Calcium	23.8mg

free from
✓ nuts
✓ dairy
✓ wheat
✓ seafood
✓ eggs
✓ yeast
✓ citrus
✓ alcohol

figs and pears in honey

SIMPLY COOKED FRUIT makes a delicious and refreshing dessert. Pears make an excellent choice as very few people have an allergic response to them.

2 Place the lemon rind, honey, cinnamon stick, cardamom pod and the water in a pan and boil, uncovered, for about 10 minutes until reduced by about half.

3 Cut the pears into eighths, discarding the core. Leave the peel on or discard as preferred. Place in the syrup, add the figs and simmer for about 5 minutes until the fruit is tender.

4 Transfer the fruit to a serving bowl. Continue cooking the liquid until syrupy, then discard the cinnamon stick and pour over the figs and pears.

INGREDIENTS

Serves four

1 lemon
90ml/6 tbsp clear honey
1 cinnamon stick
1 cardamom pod
350ml/12fl oz/1½ cups water
2 pears
8 fresh figs, halved

free from
✓ nuts
✓ dairy
✓ wheat
✓ seafood
✓ eggs
✓ yeast
  citrus
✓ alcohol

COOK'S TIP
Choose a flavourful honey for this salad – look out for one of the flower- or herb-scented varieties.

1 Pare the rind from the lemon using a zester or vegetable peeler and cut it into very thin strips usig a small sharp knife.

VARIATION
The combination of pears and figs is delightful, but in autumn and winter you could make this dessert with just pears.

NUTRITION NOTES

Per portion:

Energy	150Kcal/629kJ
Fat	0.5g
saturated fat	0g
Carbohydrate	36.5g
Fibre	3.1g
Calcium	81.5mg

spiced red fruit compote

A DELICIOUS DESSERT that is perfect in summer when fresh berries are in season. It is packed with vitamin C, which is essential for good health.

INGREDIENTS

Serves four

4 ripe red plums, halved

225g/8oz/2 cups strawberries, halved or quartered

225g/8oz/2 cups fresh or frozen raspberries

15ml/1 tbsp light brown sugar

1 cinnamon stick

3 pieces star anise

6 cloves

4 Cover the pan and let the fruit infuse over a very low heat for about 5 minutes. Remove the whole spices from the compote before serving.

COOK'S TIP

In winter, you can use frozen fruit for this dessert. It won't need extra water, as there are usually plenty of ice crystals clinging to the berries.

NUTRITION NOTES

Per portion:

Energy	62Kcal/262kJ
Fat	0.3g
saturated fat	0g
Carbohydrate	14.3g
Fibre	2.9g
Calcium	31.8mg

1 Place the fruit in a heavy pan with the sugar and 30ml/2 tbsp cold water.

2 Add the cinnamon stick, star anise and cloves to the pan.

3 Heat the fruit gently, without boiling, until the sugar dissolves and the fruit juices run.

free from

✓ nuts

✓ dairy

✓ wheat

✓ seafood

✓ eggs

✓ yeast

✓ citrus

✓ alcohol

summer fruit tofu cheesecake

THIS CREAMY CHEESECAKE is perfect for people with a dairy allergy as its made with tofu rather than cheese.

2 Tip the mixture into a 23cm/9in round flan tin (pie pan) and press down firmly. Leave to set.

3 To make the filling, place the tofu and yogurt in a food processor and process them until smooth. Soak the gelatine in the apple juice, then heat to dissolve. Stir into the tofu mixture.

4 Spread the tofu mixture over the chilled base, smoothing it evenly. Chill for an hour or two until the filling has set.

5 Carefully remove the flan tin and place the cheesecake on a serving plate.

6 Arrange the fruits on top of the cheesecake. Melt the redcurrant jelly with the hot water. Let it cool, and then spoon or brush over the fruit to serve.

INGREDIENTS

Serves six

425g/15oz tofu
300g/11oz sheep's milk yogurt
25ml/1½ tbsp/1½ sachets powdered
  gelatine
90ml/6 tbsp apple juice
175g/6oz/1¾ cups soft fruit, such as
  raspberries, strawberries and blueberries
30ml/2 tbsp redcurrant jelly
30ml/2 tbsp hot water

For the base

50g/2oz/4 tbsp dairy-free, low-fat spread
  or margarine
30ml/2 tbsp apple juice
115g/4oz/6 cups bran flakes

free from

✓ nuts
✓ dairy
　 wheat
✓ seafood
✓ eggs
　 yeast
✓ citrus
✓ alcohol

1 To make the base, place the low-fat spread or margarine and apple juice in a pan and heat them gently until the spread or margarine has melted. Crush the cereal and stir it into the juice mixture.

NUTRITION NOTES

Per portion:

Energy	181Kcal/761kJ
Fat	7.1g
saturated fat	1.9g
Carbohydrate	21.1g
Fibre	3.1g
Calcium	308.9mg

grilled pineapple with papaya sauce

BROMELAIN, AN ENZYME FOUND in pineapple, has anti-inflammatory properties and is recommended for asthmatics.

2 Line a baking sheet with foil, rolling up the sides to make a rim. Grease the foil with melted butter. Preheat the grill (broiler). Arrange the pineapple slices on the lined baking sheet. Brush with butter, then top with the ginger matchsticks, sugar and cinnamon. Drizzle over the stem ginger syrup. Grill (broil) for 5–7 minutes, or until the slices are golden and lightly charred on top.

3 Meanwhile, make the sauce. Cut a few slices from the papaya and set aside, then purée the rest with the apple juice in a food processor or blender.

4 Sieve the purée, then stir in any cooking juices from the pineapple. Serve the pineapple drizzled with the sauce and decorated with mint.

INGREDIENTS

Serves six

1 sweet pineapple
melted butter, for greasing
    and brushing
2 pieces drained stem ginger in syrup,
    cut into fine matchsticks, plus 30ml/
    2 tbsp of the syrup from the jar
30ml/2 tbsp demerara sugar
pinch of ground cinnamon
fresh mint sprigs, to decorate

For the sauce

1 ripe papaya, peeled and seeded
175ml/6fl oz/¾ cup apple juice

1 Peel the pineapple and cut spiral slices off the outside to remove the eyes. Cut it crossways into six 2.5cm/1in thick slices.

COOK'S TIP
Try the papaya sauce with grilled chicken.

NUTRITION NOTES

Per portion:	
Energy	142Kcal/594kJ
Fat	1.8g
saturated fat	0.9g
Carbohydrate	32.6g
Fibre	3g
Calcium	51.7mg

free from

✓	nuts
	dairy
✓	wheat
✓	seafood
✓	eggs
✓	yeast
✓	citrus
✓	alcohol

gooseberry and elderflower sorbet

THIS LOW-FAT, DAIRY-FREE SORBET is an excellent choice for those who are looking to avoid ice cream and dairy-based sorbets.

INGREDIENTS

Serves six

130g/4½oz/⅔ cup granulated sugar
175ml/6fl oz/¾ cup water
10 elderflower heads
500g/1¼lb/4 cups gooseberries
200ml/7fl oz/scant 1 cup apple juice
elderflowers, to decorate

1 Put 30ml/2 tbsp of the sugar in a pan with 30ml/2 tbsp of the water. Set aside. Mix the remaining sugar and water in a separate, heavy saucepan. Heat gently, stirring occasionally, until the sugar has dissolved. Bring to a boil and boil for 1 minute, without stirring, to make a syrup.

2 Remove the pan from heat and add the elderflower heads, pressing them into the syrup with a wooden spoon. Leave to infuse for about 1 hour.

3 Strain the elderflower syrup through a sieve placed over a bowl. Set the syrup aside. Add the gooseberries to the pan containing the reserved sugar and water. Cover and cook very gently for about 5 minutes, until the gooseberries have softened.

4 Transfer to a food processor and add the apple juice. Process until smooth, then press through a sieve into a bowl. Let cool. Stir in the elderflower syrup and chill until very cold.

5 If making by hand, pour the mixture into a shallow container and freeze until thick, preferably overnight. If using an ice cream maker, churn the mixture until it holds its shape. Transfer to a freezerproof container and freeze for several hours or overnight. Scoop the sorbet carefully into the glasses, decorate with elderflowers and serve.

NUTRITION NOTES

Per portion:

Energy	114Kcal/485kJ
Fat	0.4g
saturated fat	0g
Carbohydrate	28.6g
Fibre	2g
Calcium	31.2mg

raspberry sorbet

THIS MOUTHWATERING DESSERT is low in fat and rich in vitamin C, which can help to eliminate histamines, boost the immune system and reduce inflammation.

5 After this time, beat it again. If using an ice cream maker, churn the mixture until it is thick but too soft to scoop. Scrape into a freezerproof container.

6 Crush the remaining raspberries between your fingers and add them to the partially frozen ice cream. Mix lightly, then return the ice cream to the freezer for a further 2–3 hours until firm. Scoop the ice cream into dishes and serve with the extra raspberries.

INGREDIENTS

Serves six

150g/5oz/¾ cup granulated sugar
150ml/5fl oz/⅔ cup water
500g/1¼lb/3 cups raspberries, plus extra to serve
450g/1lb/2 cups virtually fat-free fromage frais

1 Put the sugar and water in a pan and bring to the boil, stirring until the sugar has dissolved. Leave to cool.

2 Put 425g/15oz/2½ cups of the raspberries in a food processor or blender. Process into a purée, then press through a sieve placed over a large bowl to remove the seeds. Stir the sugar syrup into the raspberry purée and chill the mixture until it is very cold.

3 Add the fromage frais to the purée and whisk until smooth.

4 If making by hand, pour the mixture into a plastic or other freezerproof container and freeze for 4 hours, beating once with a fork, electric beater or in a food processor to break up the ice crystals.

COOK'S TIP

If you intend to make this in an ice cream maker, check your handbook before you begin churning as this recipe makes 800g/1¾lb/3¼ cups of mixture. If this is too much for your machine, make it in two batches or by hand.

NUTRITION NOTES

Per portion:	
Energy	163Kcal/693kJ
Fat	0.4g
saturated fat	0.1g
Carbohydrate	35.2g
Fibre	2.1g
Calcium	91.4mg

free from

✓	nuts
	dairy
✓	wheat
✓	seafood
✓	eggs
✓	yeast
✓	citrus
✓	alcohol

coconut ice cream

RICH AND CREAMY COCONUT MILK is the perfect alternative for anyone avoiding cow's milk or cream.

2 Grate the limes finely, taking care to avoid the bitter pith. Squeeze them and pour the juice and rind into the pan of syrup. Add the coconut milk to the lime syrup in the pan.

3 If making by hand, pour the mixture into a plastic or other freezerproof container and freeze for 5–6 hours until firm, beating twice with a fork, electric beater or in a food processor to break up the crystals.

4 If using an ice cream maker, churn the mixture until firm enough to scoop.

5 Scoop the ice cream into wide glasses or small dishes and decorate with the toasted coconut shavings.

INGREDIENTS

Serves four

150ml/¼ pint/⅔ cup water
90g/3½oz/½ cup granulated sugar
2 limes
400ml/14fl oz can coconut milk
toasted coconut shavings, to decorate
   (see Cook's Tip)

free from

✓ nuts
✓ dairy
✓ wheat
✓ seafood
✓ eggs
✓ yeast
  citrus
✓ alcohol

COOK'S TIP

Use the flesh from a coconut to make a pretty decoration. Rinse the flesh with cold water and cut off thin slices using a vegetable peeler. Toast the slices under a medium grill until the coconut has curled and turned golden.

1 Put the water in a small pan. Add the sugar and bring to the boil, stirring constantly, until the sugar has all dissolved. Remove the pan from heat and leave the syrup to cool, then chill well.

NUTRITION NOTES

Per portion:

Energy	280Kcal/1178kJ
Fat	19.2g
saturated fat	16.4g
Carbohydrate	26.8g
Fibre	0.6g
Calcium	43.5mg

damson ice

TRY THIS WONDERFULLY SIMPLE dessert for the perfect end to any meal. Enjoy it when damsons are in season.

INGREDIENTS

Serves six

500g/1¼lb/2¼ cups ripe damsons, washed
450ml/¾ pint/scant 2 cups water
130g/4½oz/⅔ cup granulated sugar

1 Put the damsons into a pan and add 150ml/¼ pint/⅔ cup of the water. Cover and simmer for 10 minutes or until the damsons are tender

2 Pour the remaining water into a second pan. Add the sugar and bring to the boil, stirring until the sugar has dissolved. Pour the syrup into a bowl, leave to cool, then chill.

3 Break up the cooked damsons in the pan with a wooden spoon and scoop out any stones (pits). Pour the fruit and juices into a large sieve set over a bowl. Press the fruit through the sieve and discard the skins and any remaining stones from the sieve.

4 If making by hand, pour the damson purée into a shallow plastic container. Stir in the syrup and freeze for 6 hours, beating once or twice to break up the ice crystals. If using an ice cream maker, mix the purée with the syrup and churn until firm enough to scoop.

5 Spoon the ice cream into tall glasses or dishes and serve immediately.

VARIATIONS

Apricot ice can be made in the same way. Flavour the water ice with cinnamon by adding a broken cinnamon stick to the pan when poaching the fruit.

NUTRITION NOTES

Per portion:

Energy	114Kcal/473kJ
Fat	0g
saturated fat	0g
Carbohydrate	29.9g
Fibre	1.3g
Calcium	29.1mg

free from
✓ nuts
✓ dairy
✓ wheat
✓ seafood
✓ eggs
✓ yeast
✓ citrus
✓ alcohol

further information

USEFUL ADDRESSES

AUSTRALIA

ASCIA (Australasian Society of Clinical Immunology and Allergy)
ASCIA is the peak professional body of Clinical Allergists and Immunologists in Australia and New Zealand.
PO Box 450
Balgowlah
NSW Australia 2093
Email: education@allergy.org.au
Website: www.allergy.org.au

Asthma Australia
State/Territory Asthma Foundations
Free Call: 1800 645 130
Website: www.asthmaaustralia.org.au

Food Anaphylactic Children Training Support (FACTS)
Tel: 61 29913 7793
Website: www.allergyfacts.org.au

Institute of Respiratory Medicine
University of Sydney
Tel: 61 2 9515 8710
Website: www.irm.usyd.edu.au

CANADA

Alberta Lung Association
P.O. Box 4500
Station South
Edmonton
AB T6E 6K2
Tel: 780 407 6819
Toll Free: 1 800 931 9111
   or 1 888 566 5864
Health Ed Line: 1 800 661 5864
Fax: 780-407-6829
Email: info@ab.lung.ca

Allergy Home Care Products
P.O. Box 2471
Silver Spring
MD 20915
Tel: 800 327 4382
E-mail: ahcp@aol.com
Website: www.ahcp.com

Asthma Society of Canada
130 Bridgeland Avenue, Suite 425
Toronto
Ontario, M6A 1Z4
Toll Free: 1 800 787 3880
Tel: 416 787 4050
Fax: 416 787 5807
Website: www.asthma.ca

The Food Allergy & Anaphylaxis Network
10400 Eaton Place, Suite 107
Fairfax, VA 22030-2208
Tel: 800 929 4040
Fax: 703 691 2713
E-mail: faan@foodallergy.org

The National Asthma and Allergy Network
10875 Main Street, Suite 210
Fairfax
VA 22030
Tel: 703 385 4031

Ontario Lung Association
573 King Street East, Suite 201
Toronto
Ontario M5A 4L3
Toll Free: 1 800 972-2636
Tel: 416 864 9911
e-mail: olalung@on.lung.ca

NEW ZEALAND

Asthma and Respiratory Foundation of New Zealand
National Office
P. O. Box 1459
Wellington
Tel: 04-499 4592
Email: arf@asthmanz.co.nz
Website: www.asthmanz.co.nz

Asthma New Zealand
Asthma Society Inc Auckland
581 Mt Eden Rd
Mt Eden
Tel: 09 623 0236
Email: aas@asthma-nz.org.nz

Allergy New Zealand
Box 56–117
Dominion Rd
Auckland
Helpline: 09 303 2024
Toll Free: 0 800 34 0800
Tel: 09 623 3912
Fax: 09 623 0091
Email: mail@allergy.org.nz
Website: www/help@allergy.org.nz

SOUTH AFRICA

**Allergy Society Of South
  Africa (ALLSA)**
P.O. BOX 88
Observatory, 7735
Capetown
Tel: 27 21 479019
Fax: 27 21 4480846
E-mail: allsa@gem.co.sa

UNITED KINGDOM

The British Allergy Foundation
Deepdene House
30 Bellegrove Road
Welling
Kent DA16 3PY
Helpline: 020 8303 8583
Tel: 02083038525
E-mail: allergybaf@compuserve.com
Website: www.allergyfoundation.com

The National Asthma Campaign
Providence House
Providence Place
London N1 0NT
Helpline: 0845 701 0203
Tel: 020 7226 2260
Fax: 020 7704 0740
Website: www.asthma.org.uk

**The National Asthma Campaign
  Scotland**
2a North Charlotte Street
Edinburgh EH2 4HR
Tel: 0131 226 2544
Fax: 0131 226 2401

National Eczema Society
Hill House
Highgate Hill
London N19 5NA
Helpline: 0870 241 3604
Tel: 020 7281 3553
Fax : 020 7281 6395

**NATIONAL SOCIETY FOR CLEAN AIR
& ENVIRONMENTAL PROTECTION**
Address: 163 North Street, Brighton,
  BN1 1RG
Telephone: 01273 326313
Fax: 01273 892503
E-mail: admin@nsca.org.uk
Website: www.greenchannel.com/nsca

UNITED STATES

Allergy and Asthma
Mothers of Asthmatics, Inc.
2751 Prosperity Ave., Suite 150
Fairfax, Virginia 22031
Tel: 703-641-9595
Fax: 703-573-7794
E-mail: aanma@aol.com

Allergy Control Products
Specializing in anti-allergen bedding HEPA
air purifiers and vacuum cleaners.
96 Danbury Road
Ridgefield, CT 06877
Tel: 203 438 9580
Website: www.achooallergy.com

**American Lung Association
  of California**
424 Pendleton Way
Oakland, CA 94631
Tel: 510 638 5864
Fax: 510 638 8984
E-mail: contact@california lung.org
Website: www.californialung.org

**Asthma and Allergy Foundation
  of America**
1125 15th Street N.W., Suite 502
Washington, DC 20005
Tel: 202 466 7643
Fax: 800 878 4403
Website: www.aafa.org

**The National Asthma Education
  Program**
National Heart, Lung and Blood Institute
NHLBI Information Centre
P.O. Box 30105
Bethesda
MD 20824-0105
Tel: 301 951 3260
Email: NHLBInfo@rover.nhlbi.nih.gov

index